BEGINNING YOUR FAMILY HISTORY

Seventh Edition

George Pelling

revised and updated by
Pauline Litton

Published by
COUNTRYSIDE BOOKS
in association with
THE FEDERATION OF
FAMILY HISTORY SOCIETIES

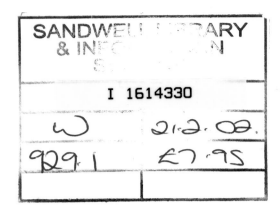

First published by FFHS 1980
Seventh edition 1998

ISBN 1 85306 550 1

COUNTRYSIDE BOOKS
3 Catherine Road
Newbury, Berkshire
and
THE FEDERATION OF
FAMILY HISTORY SOCIETIES
(PUBLICATIONS) LTD
2-4 Killer Street, Ramsbottom,
Bury, Lancs BL0 9BZ

Printed and bound at The Alden Press, Oxford

Contents

Examples

Foreword to the Seventh Edition

George Pelling was already seriously ill when he prepared the sixth edition of this book and he died only six weeks after updating the Introduction and writing, 'As always, I must express my everlasting gratitude to my beloved wife for her patience and understanding in allowing me to devote so much time to Family History. Her strength and devotion at a critical time in my life has given me the inspiration to finish this work'.

The past three years have seen so many changes in the world of family history that a new edition became essential. The increasing use of computers and the Internet, the completion of the 1881 Census Project, the improved availability of indexes ranging from FamilySearch to the General Register Office Indexes, and the relocation of several of the leading London record repositories (with more moves to come) have necessitated the insertion of several new chapters, the expansion of others and the deletion of some 'peripheral' information.

George and I first met in 1976 and were both elected as members of the executive committee of the Federation of Family History Societies on 1 April 1979. He was appointed as the first Educational Liaison Officer and it was wearing this hat that he prepared the first edition of ***Beginning Your Family History***, published in 1980 with 60 pages and a paper cover. This edition contained input from several members of the committee but it was very much George's book, using examples from his own researches to illustrate several of the chapters, and his personality was stamped even more clearly on succeeding editions.

Preparing a new edition which retains George's inimitable style (with parts of the text, particularly the Introduction, written in the first person) has not been an easy task and there are undoubtedly places where the seams show.

Information on George's ancestors has been added from the 1881 Census Project which was not published until after his death. I like to think that he would have approved of his researches being continued and updated!

This was one of the first books to include references to sources and repositories in the British Isles other than those in England and this practice has been continued. However, English information necessarily predominates and those with ancestors elsewhere will need to look to the Bibliographies for more detailed reading.

It was also one of the first books written with the beginner to family history specifically in mind. In the past eighteen years many publications on the subject have appeared but it is hoped that this one continues to fulfil George's purpose, as set out in the first edition, 'to provide some firm guide-lines to the newcomer tackling the subject for the first time'. Many of the books which treat the subject in greater detail, and which beginners will benefit from reading once they cease to be beginners, are mentioned in the text.

PML. March 1998.

Introduction to the Sixth Edition

by George Pelling

When I talk about my absorbing interest in Family History, the question sometimes arises, 'Why do you do it?'

Family History research has been described as a cross between a good detective story and a jig-saw puzzle. Certainly the thrill of the chase is experienced whilst searching and there is great satisfaction when a particularly elusive ancestor is found and put in his allotted place on the Family Tree.

Gradually changing social conditions have given rise to a society in which many people live away from their places of origin and some find it difficult to relate to their present environment. It is a natural step for them to start searching for their 'roots' and perhaps explains why family history has become so popular, particularly in America, and there is also a great interest in our other former colonies in Canada, Australia and New Zealand. There are, however, many whose families have been in the same area for generations and they obviously have a different motivation. Man has an inherent curiosity about himself and his origins and much contemporary conversation revolves around gossip about the family, neighbours and friends.

Each of us is a product of genetic and environmental influences and by studying our ancestors we can find out more about ourselves. As Don Steele wrote in 1980, '... history is not merely a chronicle of past events but an enquiry into the thoughts and actions of people in the past'. He justifiably asserts that a closer understanding of our predecessors can be achieved by studying the history of the family, the fundamental social unit, than by more traditional approaches to national and local history.

Whatever the reason, the veritable explosion of interest in the subject in recent years is remarkable. When the Federation of Family History Societies was founded in 1974 it had less than a dozen members: by 1994 this total had increased to more than 170, spread across the English speaking world. I little thought, when I wrote the introduction to the First Edition in 1980, that fourteen years (and some 80,000 copies) later, I would be writing a Sixth.

The aim of the book remains unchanged, to provide the beginner with the preliminary information necessary to research his ancestors by answering, for each main subject covered, the questions: When? What? Where? How? and Cost?. The order in which the subjects are considered will, it is hoped, help keep the costs to a minimum.

The number of ancestors doubles with each generation as you proceed backwards, four grandparents, eight great grandparents and so on, so that 10 generations back (say 300 years) you may have as many as 1,024 ancestors. Your efforts will be amply repaid by finding new relatives and if you follow the steps in this book you should be able to 'do-it-yourself'. The most rewarding aspect of this fascinating and absorbing pastime, for me, however, was unexpected. Since I set out to find my ancestors I have met many people, and have corresponded with many more, engaged on a similar quest. Although my search was in the past, I found fellowship and friendship in the present. May you be as fortunate.

Acknowledgements for the Seventh Edition

Acknowledgements for the first six editions are contained in each. The same cover has been used for all editions, except the first.

For this edition particular thanks go to:

Derek Palgrave and Colin Chapman who gave of their time and expertise as willingly for this edition as they did for the first one. Derek provided the computer-generated Line Pedigree on page 22 (having been responsible for the calligraphed version in previous editions); Colin was the originator of the Chapman County Codes reproduced on pages 37-38.

Carol McLee for reading the text (several times), for constantly reminding me that beginners cannot be assumed to know any of the things which experienced family historians take for granted, and for her knowledge of Scottish records.

Paul Gorry for his invaluable help with the Irish sections.

David Hawgood for his welcome advice on computers and the Internet.

Bob Boyd, the FFHS's production manager, for his imperturbable demeanour and his willingness, way beyond the call of duty, to cope with never-ending 'last-minute' alterations to the text.

Last but not least, my non-family historian husband for his support and encouragement. He has managed to retain his equanimity through thirty years of coping with a wife who can deal with ancestors but not with computers!

Thanks are due to the following for their kind permission to reproduce the examples used in the book:

The Corporation of the President of the Church of Jesus Christ of Latter-day Saints for the International Genealogical Index sample on page 42 and the arrangement of the 1881 census data on pages 45 and 60.

The Controller of Her Majesty's Stationery Office for the Crown copyright material in the Public Record Office (census returns on pages 45, 56, 57 and 60).

West Sussex Record Office for the Inventory on page 86.

PML.

CHAPTER ONE

The Starting Point: Family Sources

Many excellent Family Histories have been written which are sadly deficient in one respect: very little is known about the author, who assumed, modestly but wrongly, that no one was ever going to be interested in him. The golden rule is to start with yourself and work backwards, generation by generation, proving each step as far as possible by reference to the records available. These will be considered briefly in the following pages.

Do not take a person from the past with your name and try to trace his descendants in the hope that you may be one of them, even if there is a family legend that he is your ancestor. You may find, as you proceed, that your ancestral name several generations back is different from what it is today.

Family Memories

Your first sources are the memories of your immediate family and their treasures, lovingly preserved over the years. Talk to all your relatives, in particular the older generation. If you can tape-record them, do so. Be prepared to jog their memories by asking questions, but mostly listen. If recording is not possible, note what they say and try to persuade them to write down their memories. They will enjoy the experience; you will find the results fascinating reading. Memory fades and needs stimulation, so you may not obtain all the information at once. Ask some more questions after a lapse of time, when they have had the opportunity for further reflection. Bear in mind that two people's perceptions of an event or a person are rarely exactly the same. Just because your grandmother recalls something in detail, don't neglect to ask her sister what she remembers about the same happening. Your relatives may live far away and you may have to rely on correspondence. If your enquiries are vague the replies will be likewise. It is a good idea to send a questionnaire (see page 8 for example) to ensure you obtain all the essential information but make sure your relative knows who you are and why you would like these details.

If you don't understand some of the relationships which your questions produce, look at pages 10 and 11. The chart looks daunting but it is essentially very simple, provided you follow the rules step by step. You will know that first cousins have common grandparents; if you did not it can be ascertained from the chart. The key to understanding it is to substitute yourself and your relatives in place of the symbols.

Remember that today's moral code can be very different to that under which your relations grew up. The older ones – however 'liberated' they may appear – will have

	Your Name	Your Husband's/Wife's Name
Please give full names		
Previous surname(s) where appropriate		
Date/place: birth		
Date/place: marriage		
Occupation		

Your children's names *	1.	2.	3.
Date/place: birth			
Date/place: marriage			
Name of wife/husband			
Their children*	1.		
	2.		
	3.		

	Your Father	Your Mother (maiden name)
Date/place: birth/bapt		
Date/place: marriage		
Date place: death/burial		
Occupation/Religion		

Your brothers/sisters*	1.	2.	3.
Date/place: birth/bapt			
Date/place: marriage			
Name of wife/husband			
Occupation			
Their children *	1.		
* if more than three	2.		
use additional sheet	3.		

	Paternal Grandparents	Maternal Grandparents
Names		
Date/place: birth/bapt		
Date/place: marriage		
Date/place: death/burial		
Occupation/Religion		

Any other information

Your address

Telephone

Family Questionnaire Form

memories of when couples met, courted, married, acquired a house of their own and children (in that order); when illegitimacy, rushed marriages, marriage breakdowns and suicides were events to be ashamed of and never talked about; when an ancestor transported to Australia was a disgrace and not something to be eagerly sought because of the records generated by the event.

The main source of family information for my maternal grandmother's family, and the inspiration for my starting on the quest for my ancestors, was my Aunt Bess, my mother's elder, unmarried, sister, who remembered her great-grandfather, born in 1815, and told me the names of his 11 children and 65 grandchildren. It was some years, however, before she told me that she had destroyed her mother's marriage certificate, because the date was less than nine months before her own birth date.

It was 14 years afterwards, in 1984, that I finally located the Family Bible, or more accurately that the holder contacted me, via another relative. The moral is obvious: all known relatives, however remote, should be contacted. My research had not been wasted (research, even that which yields negative information, rarely is), because I was able to prove that one of the entries (which altogether covered seven generations from 1765) was inaccurate, confusion having arisen from a marriage of cousins with the same name. So, how had the error occurred? Quite simply, the bible was not published until 1846; prior entries had been made from memory, which emphasises that all sources must be checked for accuracy. Moreover, no one should be accepted as an ancestor unless and until it is proved beyond all reasonable doubt.

Family Records

Look for the following: Family Bible; Letters; Postcards and Diaries; Birth, Marriage and Death Certificates; Birthday Books; Funeral/Memorial Cards; Newspaper cuttings (often obituary notices are kept); Professional Certificates; Samplers (pieces of embroidery worked by young girls to demonstrate proficiency) and Apprenticeship Indentures, both often framed and displayed; Medals (look at the edge for name, rank and number) and Army Service Books; Ration Books; Pension Books; House Deeds; Copies of Wills; School Reports.

Photographs deserve a special mention. How many times have you looked at old photos and asked 'who do they depict'? Try to identify them and write the names lightly on the back. It is possible to reproduce old faded prints to provide a clear enlarged copy. Some photographers will do this for you, and can treat any creased or torn photographs before copying to disguise the damage; good photocopiers will produce reasonable facsimiles and on modern laser copiers you can have several coloured photographs printed onto an A3 sheet for £5 or less.

Do think about the care and conservation of the family records you acquire. Many of them will have survived in good condition because they have been stored out of direct light, perhaps in the pages of a book, or at the bottom of a drawer or cupboard.

continued on page 12

Relationships

		H	1	2	3	4	5
	CA	→	C	GC	GGC	2 × GGC	3 × GGC
V	↓						
1	C		s	n	gn	ggn	2 × ggn
2	GC		n	1c	1c1r	1c2r	1c3r
3	GGC		gn	1c1r	2c	2c1r	2c2r
4	2 × GGC		ggn	1c2r	2c1r	3c	3c1r
5	3 × GGC		2 × ggn	1c3r	2c2r	3c1r	4c

Relationships Chart

The chart can be extended indefinitely: cousins will always be on the diagonal from top left to bottom right.
Note: **H** = Horizontal, **V** = Vertical (used to enable identification of squares on the two lines).

Key to Chart

CA = Common Ancestor.
Relationship with Common Ancestor: **C** = Child: **GC** = Grandchild: **GGC** = Great-Grandchild:
Number **x** = times Great (so 3 x **GGC** = Great-Great-Great Grandchild).
Relationship between relatives with a common ancestor:
s = sibling (brother or sister)
n = nephew/niece:
c = cousin
gn = great-nephew/niece (alternatively known as grand-nephew/niece)
number **r** = times removed (e.g. **1c1r** = first cousin once removed).

The following abridged Family Tree shows Alfred and Annie, who are the common ancestors of their daughters, Margaret and Nora; their grandchildren, George and Alice; and their great-grandchildren, Nichola and Janet.

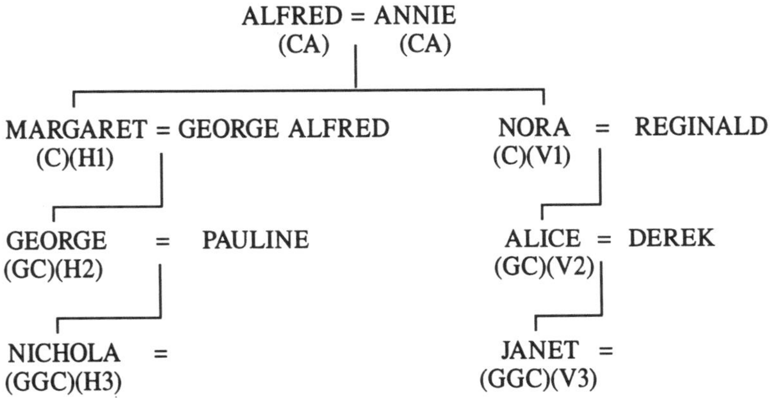

The application of the chart to the persons on the tree will demonstrate how it works.

1. George and Alice have common grandparents; therefore, place George at H2 = GC and Alice at V2 = GC. Their relationship is stated where columns H2 and V2 intersect, i.e. 1c [first cousin].
2. What is the relationship of George to Alice's daughter Janet? They are not second cousins, as is commonly supposed. George is H2 [GC], Janet is V3 [GGC]: H2 and V3 intersect at 1c1r = first cousin once removed. Logical enough, since Janet is one generation removed from George's first cousin Alice. It is Nichola and Janet who are second cousins.

A word of warning: relationships may not be what they seem. Those on the Chart are all blood relations (kin) but their titles are extended to those on the Family Tree 'by marriage' so George would customarily call his aunt Nora's husband 'uncle Reg' and Margaret would refer to her niece Alice's husband as her nephew; Janet (and her children) might well refer to George as 'uncle' rather than 'cousin'.

Until recent times a friend or neighbour (kith) might be given the honorary title of 'aunt' or 'uncle' – there are those of us who remember when close friends of our parents were always called this because we were not allowed to use the forenames of our elders.

In modern parlance, Reginald is Margaret's brother-in-law but for another common meaning of 'in-law' in the past see Chapter 9.

Try to remember, when questioning relatives and friends, to ask whether the relationship is by blood, by marriage, or merely a courtesy title.

continued from page 9

It would be tragic if they deteriorated rapidly just because you didn't take good care of them. Photographs should be kept out of direct light, especially sunlight, or they will quickly fade (this applies particularly to early colour photographs). The same applies to photocopies of documents. All papers should be kept in special acid-free folders, obtainable from any good stationer. Some of the cheaper plastic 'pockets' positively encourage the printing (whether old powder-based, or modern photocopying, inks or photographic emulsion) to leave their paper and stick to the cellulose.

Gravestones

Try to find out where your ancestors were buried. Gravestones are an invaluable source for clarifying family relationships and often include information about several generations, which may save you the cost of purchasing some certificates. Stones become worn and the older ones are difficult to read. Record what you can, leaving spaces where words are not clear, and indicate where you have made a guess.

e.g. JOHN SMITH(ER?)S died January (?)th 18(53?), Aged 6(5?)

Look for graves in the vicinity bearing the same surname. Relatives often purchased adjacent plots.

Until the 19th century most people were buried in the local churchyard. The first burial grounds for Nonconformists (i.e. not of the Established Church) were opened in the 17th century and increased in number in the 18th. The first public cemeteries appeared in the early 1800s as private ventures but most date from the 1850s or later. Some have well indexed records.

Public cemeteries are maintained by local authorities and not by the Church.The records for a cemetery still in use will normally be found at the Office at the cemetery but some records may be held in Borough Council Offices. The register will normally record dates of death and burial, in addition to name, address, occupation and age of the deceased and possibly an indication that other relatives are buried in the grave. A grave number will be given, from which the plot can be located from the grave plan and other occupants of the grave identified. The cemetery's address will usually be found in the telephone directory, often listed under the local authority's Leisure and Amenity Services. Be aware that occasionally a fee may be charged for information.

Recognising their unique value, family history societies and other public spirited organisations, as well as dedicated individuals, have recorded Monumental (or Memorial) Inscriptions (MIs). The recordings are usually indexed, which saves valuable searching time, and an increasing number are being published and sold, mainly by family history societies. Your local library may have a copy of those within its area. The Society of Genealogists (SoG) has built up a substantial collection for its library in London.

If the churchyard or burial ground in which your ancestor was buried has been landscaped, or otherwise destroyed, the inscriptions may (should, if after 1906) have been recorded, although often in a disappointingly brief manner. Again your local library may have a copy. Bear in mind that gravestones were never erected over many graves and that it is only within about the last hundred years that most ordinary families have been able to afford to erect a stone. The increasing popularity of cremation means that MIs will be much less common in future.

To help family historians find the burials of their ancestors, the majority of family history societies in the British Isles are extracting and indexing entries from Parish Registers and Nonconformist records as part of the National Burials Index project being organised by the Federation of Family History Societies. The aim of this project is eventually to provide a search facility for burials similar to that for baptisms and marriages as found in the International Genealogical Index (see Chapter 7). Most societies, in return for a reasonable fee, will provide a search service of their database and many, as sections of work are completed for their areas, are compiling booklets or microfiche for sale.

Dates on tombstones (like dates in most records) cannot be relied upon as the stone may have been erected years after the first interment. Do remember that the stone is a memorial which means that not all those listed may be buried there (and therefore they will not be recorded in the burial registers) and that the last member of a generation to die may be in the grave but not mentioned on the stone because there was no one left to arrange for the name to be added.

Bibliography

Basic Facts about Sources for Family History in the Home, Iain Swinnerton. FFHS, 1995.

Family History in Focus, ed. Don Steel and Lawrence Taylor. Lutterworth Press, 1984.

Dating Old Photographs, 2nd edition, Robert Pols. FFHS, 1995.

Understanding Old Photographs, Robert Pols. Robert Boyd Publications, 1995.

Rayment's Notes on Recording Monumental Inscriptions, 4th edition, revised by Penelope Pattinson. FFHS, 1992.

See also Bibliography to Chapter Seven.

CHAPTER TWO

Setting Your Sights

Being Selective

Start immediately to fill in an Ancestor Chart (sometimes called a Pedigree Chart or Birth Brief) as far back as you can. A sample chart is shown on page 16, which provides spaces for all your ancestors back to your 16 great-great-grandparents. Most family history societies will be able to supply copies of similar ones. The most important thing to decide next is which of the possible options you should choose, otherwise you will simply be ancestor collecting with no objective in view. Your choice will be influenced by the data you have immediately available. You may, of course, change your mind later, when you have obtained more material and as you become increasingly familiar with family history, but you should be aware of the following possibilities at an early stage, since this may influence your approach.

One Name Study

The researcher collects every reference to a particular surname, wherever and whenever it occurs.

Total Ancestry

Having traced 16 great-great-grandparents, the researcher then looks for their 32 parents, so that every time one ancestor is found he starts looking for two more.

Several Families

The researcher investigates a number of families (perhaps those of his four grandparents) in depth, by putting them into their local and historical context with, perhaps, the ultimate aim of writing a family history (see Chapter 15).

Seeking Help

The previously stated aim of this book is to show you how to do it yourself but, however independent and dedicated you may be, you will need help.

Libraries

Visit your local library, with which you may already be familiar (though perhaps not with the Reference section), where you will find copies of at least some of the material mentioned in the following pages. If your library has a Local History/Local Studies section, see Chapter 5 for brief details of what it may hold. Library books are arranged under code numbers: those listed and many others useful to a family historian will be found under code 929. Remember that if your library does not hold a book which you require, a copy can usually be ordered, for a small fee, via the inter-library loan service. The library notice board or a member of staff should have details of local societies and particulars of any further education classes covering the subject of family history.

A list of helpful books appears at the end of each chapter. Those at the end of this one generally cover the same ground as this book but in much more detail; those included in other chapters are usually more specialised publications dealing with particular subjects. For books dealing specifically with research in Wales, Scotland and Ireland see the Bibliography to Chapter 5.

Family History Societies

There is almost certainly a family history society covering the area in which you live and membership subscriptions are modest (usually £5-£10 per annum). You do not have to be an expert to join; everyone is welcome, especially beginners. Your ancestors may be from a different part of the country and you may feel that your local society is remote from your areas of interest, but most societies produce a quarterly journal, and exchange copies with similar societies, thus building up a library of material from outside their immediate region. Additionally, most societies hold monthly meetings (except, perhaps, for a summer break) and have speakers on a variety of subjects, national as well as local. Most importantly, you will meet fellow family historians who have experienced the same problems and may be able to help you overcome them. I write from personal experience: in 1973 my employer decided that my services were required in Lancashire. I have no known ancestors north of Felixstowe but joined the local Rossendale Society, of which I successively became Treasurer, Projects Co-ordinator, Chairman and Vice-President.

Mention has already been made of the Federation of Family History Societies and a current list of member societies is included on the back cover of its journal ***Family History News and Digest,*** which is published twice a year, in April and September. Alternatively, the Administrator of the FFHS (c/o The Benson Room, Birmingham & Midland Institute, Margaret Street, Birmingham B3 3BS) will provide a copy of the list in return for an s.a.e. (see below). The address of the society secretary may not be close to where you live but do not let that deter you from seeking further information; most societies have more than one meeting venue, some of the larger ones have as many as 11 branches. For example the old county of Lancashire is covered by seven societies, which between them have more than 20 meeting places. As well as joining a society close to your home, it is recommended that you join one which covers the area in which your ancestors lived. You may not be able to attend more than the occasional meeting but the society will have members with a wealth of local knowledge and most will have indexes and transcripts of local Monumental Inscriptions, Parish Registers and other sources mentioned in this book which you will be able to consult by post.

There are ever growing numbers of One Name Societies and individuals who specialise in particular surnames. To find out whether yours is amongst the thousands

continued on page 18

N.B. It follows that all even numbers are male, and all odd (above 1) female.

SELF

1 George Pelling
BORN 25 Jun 1933
WHERE Ockley Sry
WHEN MARRIED 19 Aug 1961
WHERE West Blatchington Ssx

NAME OF HUSBAND OR WIFE
Pauline Winifrid Holden

PARENTS

FATHER
2 George Alfred Pelling
BORN 11 Apr 1895
WHERE Dorking Sry
WHEN MARRIED 1 Oct 1932
WHERE MARRIED Portslade Ssx
DIED 22 Mar 1970
WHERE Brighton Ssx

MOTHER
3 Margaret R. Passifull
BORN 26 Jul 1904
WHERE Portslade Ssx
DIED 14 Oct 1984
WHERE Chichester Ssx

GRANDPARENTS

FATHER'S FATHER
4 Alexander Pelling
BORN 10 Jul 1855
WHERE Ewhurst Sry
WHEN MARRIED 13 Jan 1895
WHERE MARRIED Dorking Sry
DIED 23 Nov 1936
WHERE Ockley Sry

FATHER'S MOTHER
5 Sarah Jane Penfold
BORN 28 Jan 1863
WHERE Ifield Ssx
DIED 2 Dec 1951
WHERE Ockley Sry

MOTHER'S FATHER
6
BORN
WHERE
WHEN MARRIED
WHERE MARRIED
DIED
WHERE

MOTHER'S MOTHER
7
BORN
WHERE
DIED
WHERE

GT. GRANDPARENTS

FATHER OF 4
8 Michael Pelling
BAPT 18 Jun 1818
WHERE Rudgwick Ssx
WHEN MARRIED 17 Mar 1846
DIED 17 Apr 1861
WHERE Ewhurst Sry

MOTHER OF 4
9 Ann Burfoot
BAPT 13 Jan 1819
WHERE Horsham Ssx
DIED
WHERE

10
BORN
WHERE
WHEN MARRIED
DIED
WHERE

11
BORN
WHERE
DIED
WHERE

12
BORN
WHERE
WHEN MARRIED
DIED
WHERE

13
BORN
WHERE
DIED
WHERE

14
BORN
WHERE
WHEN MARRIED
DIED
WHERE

15
BORN
WHERE
DIED
WHERE

GT. GT. GRANDPARENTS

FATHER OF 8
16 Jose (Joshua) Pelling

MOTHER OF 8
17 Hannah Bridger

18

19

20

21

22

23

24

25

26

27

28

29

30

31

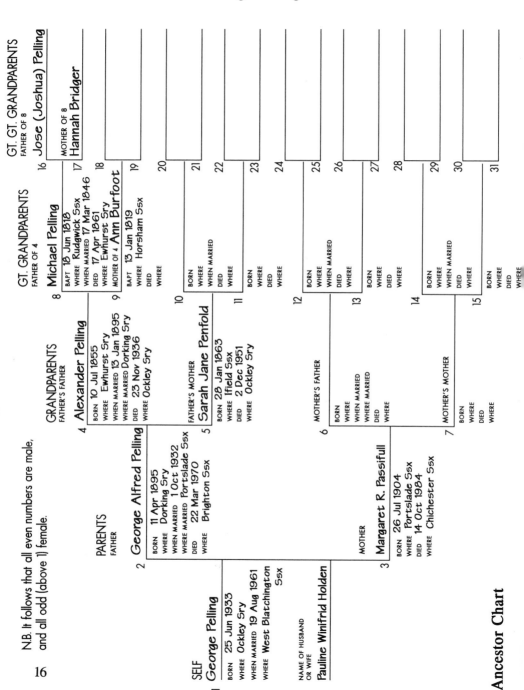

Ancestor Chart

FAMILY GROUP SHEET

NAME **Michael Pelling** REF. NO. ________

Event	Date	Place	Source
Born			
Baptism	18 Jun 1818	Rudgwick, Ssx	Parish Register
Marriage 1	17 Mar 1846	Horsham, Ssx	Mar. Cert.
Marriage 2.			
Marriage 3.			
Died	17 Apr 1861	Ewhurst, Sry	Death Cert.
Buried			
Occupation	Beerhouse Keeper (1851) Labourer (1861)		Census and Cert.
Will/Admon			
Father	Jose (Joshua) Pelling		Parish Register
Mother	Hannah Bridger		Parish Register
Spouse 1	Ann Burfoot (m. 2 Edward Whenham)		Mar. Cert.
Spouse 2			
Spouse 3			

Children in order of birth

	Name		Born		At	Source	Chart No.
1.	Sidney	born	c1847	at	Horsham	1851 census	
2.	Hannah	born	c1849	at	Horsham	1851 census	
3.	Ann	born	1850	at	Horsham	1851 census	
4.	George	born	c1853	at	Ewhurst	1881 census	
5.	Alexander	born	10 Jul 1855	at	Ewhurst	Birth cert	
6.	Richard	born	c1857	at	Ewhurst	1881 census	
7.	Elizabeth	born	1860/1	at	Ewhurst	1861 census	
8.		born		at			
9.		born		at			
10.		born		at			

Family Group Sheet.

continued from page 15

now covered, apply to The Registrar, Guild of One-Name Studies, Box G, 14 Charterhouse Buildings, Goswell Road, London EC1M 7BA for a copy of their prospectus.

Postage

When writing to anyone from whom a reply is required you should enclose a reasonable-sized stamped, addressed envelope (s.a.e.) or, if writing to or from overseas, send at least two International Reply Coupons (IRCs), obtainable from most Post Offices. S.a.e. and IRC are abbreviations which you will come across frequently in family history research so it is worth explaining a little further. S.a.e. is the term used in the United Kingdom to mean stamped, addressed envelope but, in some countries overseas, s.a.e. means self-addressed envelope and s.a.s.e. means self-addressed, stamped envelope; if in doubt include a stamp! Do bear in mind that you cannot use a stamp from your own country when sending an s.a.e. to another country, you must enclose IRCs. Most of us have a collection of envelopes bearing American or Australasian (or Irish, Channel Islands or Isle of Man) stamps which we cannot use! An IRC is a voucher which can be purchased in almost any country in the world and exchanged elsewhere for stamps to cover the minimum airmail postage to the country to which the envelope is addressed. The basic rate of airmail postage in the UK only covers letters weighing 10 grams (one sheet of ordinary weight paper) so it is usually advisable to send at least two IRCs.

Bibliography

Tracing Your Family Tree, Jean Cole & John Titford. Countryside Books, 1997

Tracing Your British Ancestors, 2nd edition, C.R.Chapman. Lochin Publishing, 1996.

An Introduction to Planning Research: Short Cuts in Family History, Michael Gandy. FFHS, 1993.

Family Tree Detective, 3rd edition, Colin Rogers. Manchester University Press, 1998.

Genealogical Research in England and Wales, (3 vols.), David E. Gardner and Frank Smith. Salt Lake City, 1956-1964. [dated in parts but still extremely valuable]

The Family Historian's Enquire Within, 5th edition, Pauline Saul. FFHS, 1995. (This is virtually an encyclopaedia for family historians. A hard-back version entitled *Tracing your Ancestors: The A-Z Guide,* is published by Countryside Books.)

The Dictionary of Genealogy: a guide to British ancestry research, 4th edition, T. Fitzhugh, revised by Susan Lumas on behalf of the SoG. A & C Black, 1994.

CHAPTER THREE

Handling Data

The face of family history and, in particular, the methods of collecting, handling and storing information (data) have changed almost beyond recognition in the last twenty five years. When this book was conceived, it was still possible to view the original census enumerators' books in the Public Record Office, most Parish Registers were still in the churches, microfilm was not common, microfiche almost unknown, indexes were compiled by writing out thousands of slips of paper and sorting them into an alphabetical sequence by hand and the International Genealogical Index (IGI), then known as the Computer File Index, was hardly heard of outside America. The advent of computers and the tremendous upsurge in the production of records on microform (film or fiche) has transformed the situation.

Computers

Many family historians use computers, email or the Internet; to write letters seeking facts or advice, to store and organise information, and later possibly to write up and publish their results. There are hundreds of commercially-written programs to help this process. Some concentrate on entering information about people you know to be related, and the sources of information, then provide a variety of ways of printing charts and family trees. Often you can include family photographs on the trees. Others concentrate on the research process; you can enter information about a variety of people, some of whom may be related and others who happen to have the same surname, and use the computer to help sort them out.

Information about particular programs is in the books in the Bibliography and there are usually some being demonstrated and on sale at Family History Fairs.

Once you have keyed information into such a program, you can almost always transfer it to other programs; they use a standard for information transfer called GEDCOM to make this possible. This means that the initial choice of program is not critical – it is better to buy one and use it rather than spend a long time deciding which is best for your purposes.

Use of the Internet is becoming a good way to contact other researchers, to find out about places where your ancestors lived, and what records are available. So far only a very small proportion of records are available for searching on the Internet, but see Chapters 5 and 14 for more information. More are available on CD-ROM and you may find these on computers in a local library.

Recording Information

The Ancestor Chart, already considered in Chapter 2, only has sufficient space to record the essential data of birth/baptism, marriage, death/burial, with the dates of each. Other information can be included on Family Group Sheets, as illustrated on page 17.

You will, however, collect a lot of other material and secondary records will be necessary. No two family historians will ever agree about the best methods of recording additional information but some generally agreed principles can be stated:

(a) Start recording your information immediately.
(b) Be methodical and be honest. Acknowledge family indiscretions.
(c) Always identify your source and the date on which you made your search.
(d) A research record is as essential as a statement of the results.

List source searched, dates covered and the names for which you have looked, plus place and date of search:

e.g. Parish Register of Rudgwick (Ssx); Baps & Mars 1760-1812, Burs 1781-1812. All PELLING entries: BRIDGER entries pre-1802. 3 Dec [19]80. West Sussex Record Office (Microfilm).

This example illustrates some other recommended practices:

(i) Use capital letters for surnames, particularly vital for families where surnames are also used as christian names.

(ii) Ssx = Sussex. Place names should indicate the county, in case of duplication elsewhere. For example, you know that the Preston you researched was in Lancashire but it might not be obvious to anyone following, who might have to consider the 20 or more places of that name in other counties. For county abbreviations you are recommended to use the Chapman County Codes (see Chapter 6).

(iii) Conventional abbreviations (see Chapter 6) have been used in noting the records. This practice should not, however, be extended to the names you write down. Jo., found in an archive, should be recorded as such, not as John or Joseph, because that is what you think it means. It could be one of those or equally well be an abbreviation of Jonas, Jonathan, Joshua or Josiah. Similarly, it is not advisable to shorten names as you extract them from the archive. You might remember that you used Jo. for John and Jn. for Jonathan but anyone else reading your notes could well interpret them as Joshua and John. When recording surnames, always make it very clear on **every** page of your notes which name you are dealing with. It is all too easy to use just the first letter to save time and later to look at a page of Ps and be unable to remember whether on that occasion you were recording Pelling, Parsifall or Penfold, or to drop your notes on the floor with the same effect!

(iv) When recording dates you are advised to use letters for the month, not a number. 3/12/80 means 3 Dec[ember] 1980 in the UK but 12 Mar[ch] 1980 in America and a discrepancy of nine months could make a considerable difference to an interpretation of your family tree. Dates in computer generated records are shown in numbers in the sequence year/month/day. For an explanation of the system of double dating see page 64; for the system used by the Quakers see page 77.

(e) It is just as important to record negative results. e.g. MIs [Monumental Inscriptions] St. James, Haslingden (Lancs) 23 Sep 1979; No MUSKIES.

(f) Whatever system you adopt for recording your data – whether paper, computer or a combination of the two – must be flexible so that additional information can be added, as found. A loose leaf paper system is therefore recommended and a ring binder larger than A4 will probably be required to accommodate the larger documents and photocopies you may expect to accumulate. Beyond this stage, some family historians remain faithful to various forms of the traditional card index while others rely totally on their computers. This is a personal decision.

(g) Records must be cross-referenced. Details of family groups should be kept separate from each other, either in distinct sections of the folder or file, or in separate folders. The same people will occur in both sections (a husband's section will contain the name of his wife and vice versa) and you need to be able to refer easily from one to the other.

Family Trees

Some people are content with Ancestor Charts and Family Group Sheets as shown on pages 16 and 17 (whether on paper or computer) and never bother to put their information into what is commonly called 'family tree form'. A number of firms produce elaborate charts on which you can enter up to 256 direct ancestors (eight generations apart from yourself) and many people go no further than this. In the past many family historians shied away from drawing family trees (often called drop-line pedigrees, for obvious reasons) because of the severe problems of draughtsmanship involved but this should no longer be a hurdle. Anyone who uses a computer for their family history will find that constructing family trees is easy and those who do not use modern technology will find plenty of people advertising in family history magazines who are willing, for a fee, either to input information to produce such a tree or to use calligraphy to draw one.

The line pedigree (see page 22) is the most used format, either showing the direct line only or, in a more detailed form, including all the children of the couples involved (as with the last line on page 22). Many of the pitfalls of confusion which may arise can be avoided if, once again, certain basic rules are followed:

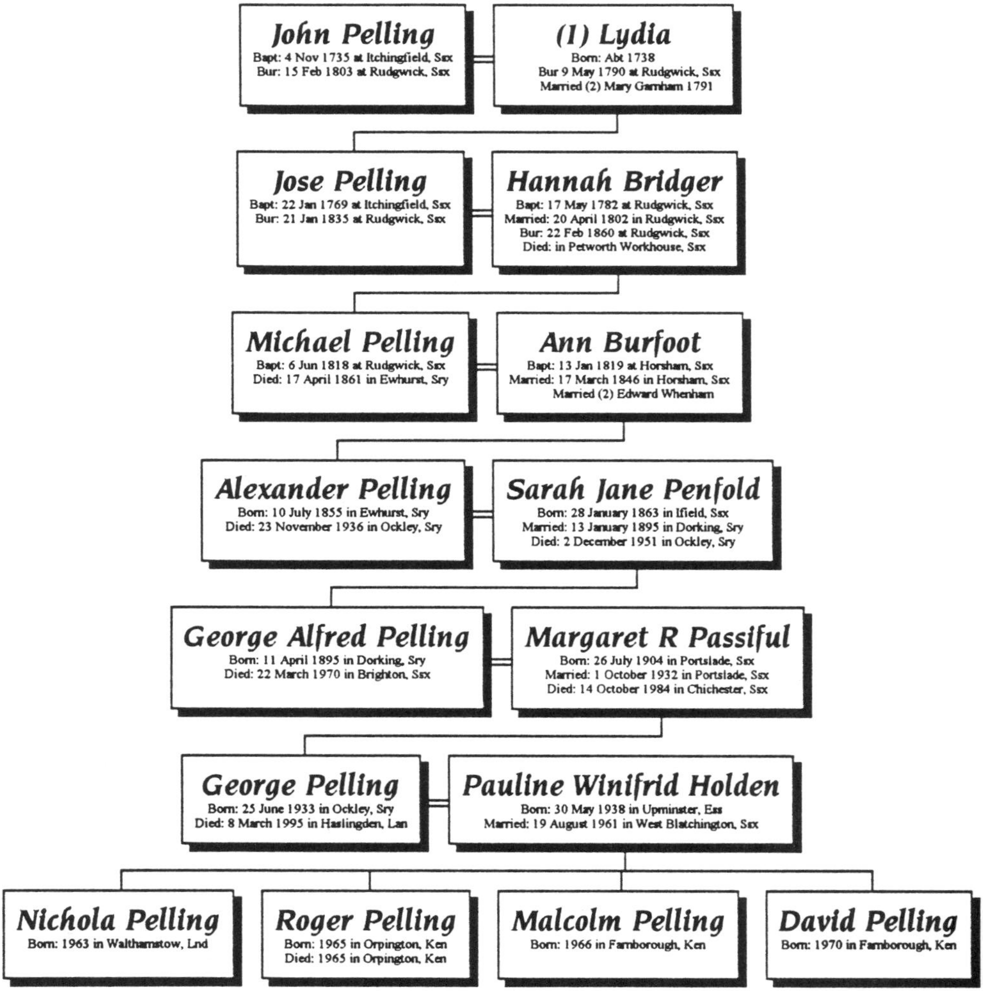
John Pelling
Bapt: 4 Nov 1735 at Itchingfield, Ssx
Bur: 15 Feb 1803 at Rudgwick, Ssx
(1) Lydia
Born: Abt 1738
Bur 9 May 1790 at Rudgwick, Ssx
Married (2) Mary Garnham 1791
Jose Pelling
Bapt: 22 Jan 1769 at Itchingfield, Ssx
Bur: 21 Jan 1835 at Rudgwick, Ssx
Hannah Bridger
Bapt: 17 May 1782 at Rudgwick, Ssx
Married: 20 April 1802 in Rudgwick, Ssx
Bur: 22 Feb 1860 at Rudgwick, Ssx
Died: in Petworth Workhouse, Ssx
Michael Pelling
Bapt: 6 Jun 1818 at Rudgwick, Ssx
Died: 17 April 1861 in Ewhurst, Sry
Ann Burfoot
Bapt: 13 Jan 1819 at Horsham, Ssx
Married: 17 March 1846 in Horsham, Ssx
Married (2) Edward Whenham
Alexander Pelling
Born: 10 July 1855 in Ewhurst, Sry
Died: 23 November 1936 in Ockley, Sry
Sarah Jane Penfold
Born: 28 January 1863 in Ifield, Ssx
Married: 13 January 1895 in Dorking, Sry
Died: 2 December 1951 in Ockley, Sry
George Alfred Pelling
Born: 11 April 1895 in Dorking, Sry
Died: 22 March 1970 in Brighton, Ssx
Margaret R Passiful
Born: 26 July 1904 in Portslade, Ssx
Married: 1 October 1932 in Portslade, Ssx
Died: 14 October 1984 in Chichester, Ssx
George Pelling
Born: 25 June 1933 in Ockley, Sry
Died: 8 March 1995 in Haslingden, Lan
Pauline Winifrid Holden
Born: 30 May 1938 in Upminster, Ess
Married: 19 August 1961 in West Blatchington, Ssx
Nichola Pelling
Born: 1963 in Walthamstow, Lnd
Roger Pelling
Born: 1965 in Orpington, Ken
Died: 1965 in Orpington, Ken
Malcolm Pelling
Born: 1966 in Farnborough, Ken
David Pelling
Born: 1970 in Farnborough, Ken

Line Pedigree

1. Names of the same generation should be kept at the same level.
2. Brief narrative information may be added below the name, but the whole purpose and effect of the line pedigree is nullified if it is cluttered with too much detail, which is better recorded elsewhere.
3. Conventionally, lines of descent are drawn from the marriage symbol (see page 11), although some computer programs deviate from this (see opposite).
4. If descent is not displayed in detail (for example, if details of a couple and their children are shown on a separate page) use an arrow under the marriage.
5. Where there is more than one marriage, clearly indicate that fact next to the marriage symbol.

   e.g. = (1) indicates one or more further marriages.
   = (2) indicates that the marriage on the pedigree is a second marriage.
6. If there is no marriage (and it does happen!) the line of illegitimate descent is shown by a broken (dots or dashes or slashed) line; if the name of the father is unknown, the line of descent is placed under the centre of the mother's name.
7. Normally record children in strict order of birth, from left to right. However, it may be necessary to depart from this rule (e.g. when cousins marry). If so, indicate by numbering the children, in order not to break the next rule, which should be regarded as inviolable.
8. Never, ever, create confusion by crossing pedigree lines.
9. Record only information which has been verified. Do not include material copied from printed sources unless you have checked, as far as possible, the original sources. If simply copied, this should be stated: e.g. from (*title of publication* and its date), or from IGI. It is often, however, helpful to pencil names on a chart and then ink them in when the information is verified.

Bibliography

Basic Facts about Keeping Your Family Records, Iain Swinnerton. FFHS, 1995.
How to Record Your Family Tree, 6th edition, Patrick Palgrave-Moore. Elvery-Dowers, 1994.
Record-Keeping for a One-Name Study, David Pulvertaft. Guild of One-Name Studies, 1990.
Basic Record Keeping for Family Historians, Andrew Todd. Allen & Todd, 1991.
Introduction to Using Computers for Genealogy, David Hawgood. FFHS, 1994.
Computers in Genealogy: Beginners' Handbook. SoG, 1994.
Web Publishing for Genealogy, Peter Christian. David Hawgood, Acton, 1997.
Internet for Genealogy, David Hawgood (author and publisher), 1996.

CHAPTER FOUR

Who Has Been Here Before Me?

At one time family historians and genealogists tended to be thought of as 'lone wolves' who preferred to work in isolation, undertaking all their own research and keeping the results to themselves. All that has changed and to-day co-operation is the name of the game. Which sources can you consult to find out not only what has been done before but also what is being done now?

Family Historians have sometimes spent years researching a family, only to discover that a substantial pedigree already exists. If you find one, however, your task is not over, it has simply been made easier. All printed and manuscript pedigrees should be checked against the original records for authenticity and accuracy and also for completeness. Many printed pedigrees were compiled in the nineteenth century when, it is probably true to say, standards of proof were lower than we would consider acceptable today. Some of the pedigrees were prepared for people of standing and 'inconvenient' ancestors may have been deliberately omitted. Although you should approach such pedigrees with the necessary scepticism, invaluable information can still be obtained from them.

Always enquire whether a record office or library has such pedigrees available. Many will be 'hidden' in the pages of local or county histories, known only to the local librarian, and may well have escaped the books mentioned below. The Society of Genealogists, 14 Charterhouse Buildings, Goswell Road, London EC1M 7BA, has a large collection of manuscript pedigrees in its substantial library.

Indexes of printed pedigrees are contained in the following books:

Index to Printed Pedigrees	C.Bridger (prior to 1867)
The Genealogist's Guide	G.W. Marshall (prior to 1903)
A Genealogical Guide	J.B. Whitmore (1900-1950)
The Genealogist's Guide	G.B. Barrow (1950-1977)

The dates in brackets indicate when the pedigrees were printed, not the dates the pedigrees cover (e.g. a pedigree from the 16th century to 1890 printed in 1956 would be indexed by Barrow and not by Marshall.)

There are many books containing printed pedigrees of the nobility and land-owning families. The best known of these are ***Burke's Peerage***, ***Debrett's Peerage*** and ***Burke's Landed Gentry,*** all of which have appeared in many editions since the 1700s (***Landed Gentry*** since 1836). Don't be put off by the thought that your ancestors were not aristocratic – many descendants of younger sons and daughters moved down the social scale, rather than up, and you may find a family connection several generations back. If you have an ancestor who achieved some distinction in his own field then he may be listed in ***Who Was Who?***, which contains biographical information, or in a publication produced by the professional body concerned, be it ***Lancashire Clocks and Clockmakers*** or ***Medical Officers in the British Army***. More detailed information may be found in the ***Dictionary of National Biography*** (now also available on CD-ROM). Most of the above can be found in any good reference library.

The largest collection of pedigrees is held in the form of Family Group Sheets (see page 17) by the Church of Jesus Christ of Latter-day Saints (commonly known as Mormons and often abbreviated to LDS or LDS Church) at their main Family History Library in Salt Lake City, Utah, USA. They are also responsible for the International Genealogical Index (IGI), details of which are given in Chapter 7.

Most family history societies periodically publish Registers of Members' Interests, which show the names being researched by their members, together with their locations and dates, and the name and address of the researcher. Many societies update their Members' Interests by printing the names being researched by new members in their journals.

There are also a number of national and international directories, produced at regular intervals, which are well worth consulting. The two which are most easily available, in libraries and record offices or for sale, are the ***British Isles Genealogical Register (BIG R)***, published on microfiche only, by the FFHS, with the first edition in 1994 and the second in 1997, and the ***National Genealogical Directory,*** published annually in book form and on CD-ROM. Both contain entries from people worldwide; BIG R lists names being researched in the British Isles by family historians worldwide, the NGD includes names being researched anywhere in the world.

Bibliography

Kelly's Handbook to the Titled, Landed and Official Classes (from 1874); later ***Kelly's Handbook of Distinguished People***

Debrett's Handbook of Distinguished People in British Life (1982)

Crockford's Clerical Directory [Anglican Clergymen] (from 1858)

Who's Who (from 1848)

Genealogical Bibliographies, Stuart Raymond.

(An on-going series of County Bibliographies containing details of printed works relating to the county which are likely to be of use to family historians; some 20 counties have been dealt with to date.)

CHAPTER FIVE

Record Repositories: National and Local

General Information

Once you have collected information from relatives and from your local library, you will need to consider visiting a record office or record repository. Many people think of these as places which hold only original records and documents. The term is used here in a wider sense, to mention the main holders of collections of material, in whatever form, which may be of use to a family historian.

You are advised to obtain a copy of the leaflet ***You and Your Record Office,*** available from the FFHS in return for an s.a.e. and an extra 1st class stamp. Some repositories have limited space available for researchers so do not assume that you can be accommodated; to avoid disappointment always write or telephone first to ascertain:

(i) If the record you want is available and, if so, in what form. Many of the books and papers you wish to consult will be produced for you only in microform, whether it be microfilm, microfiche or CD-ROM.

(ii) If it is necessary to book a place (seat or microform reader or both) and if one is available on the day of your proposed visit. Be assured that microform readers are easy to operate and staff should show you how to use them as well as explaining how to access films or fiche if the office, centre or library has a self-service system.

(iii) If you will need to produce identification before being admitted and, if so, which documents are acceptable; one showing a current address is generally preferred. Passports do not meet the requirements at some repositories.

(iv) If you are disabled, or have difficulty climbing stairs, ask what facilities the office has. Some, particularly the more modern ones, have good accommodation for the disabled, others make little provision for them.

(v) If you are permitted to take handbags, briefcases or outer garments into the search rooms – some offices do not allow this.

(vi) If they have published a list of their holdings of Parish Registers, Bishops' Transcripts and other documents. These, which can be purchased and studied in advance of a visit, are invaluable if you anticipate doing a lot of research in a particular area.

Using Record Offices

Parish Registers (and any other original documents which you may be permitted to consult) are irreplaceable and vulnerable, so always treat them with respect by observing the following rules.

Whilst examining records:

(i) **ALWAYS USE PENCIL – never** ink or ball-point pen.
(ii) **Do not** eat, drink, smoke or chew.
(iii) **Do not** rest anything on the document, or run a finger or pencil down it. **NEVER** attempt to copy by tracing, unless you have permission and use a sheet of perspex to protect the document.
(iv) Turn pages carefully.
(v) Leave the document as you found it, in the sequence in which it was filed.

When using a microform (film or fiche) reader:

(i) Always rewind the film when you have finished with it; some repositories 'fix' one reel to make sure you do this.
(ii) If you leave the machine for more than a minute or two, **switch it off.** Bulbs are expensive and they can burn out surprisingly quickly.
(iii) Always observe the repository's rules for returning films or fiche! If one is re-filed incorrectly it can take, literally, hours to locate it.

Remember that you are an ambassador for those who come to research after you; the reception they receive may be coloured by what you have done, or failed to do. One bad impression will last longer than many good ones.

It is essential that all preparatory work be done prior to visiting a record office; make sure that adequate notes are taken with you, plus a folder and notepaper. Staff at most record offices do not have the time to assist you with detailed enquiries when you visit personally but many offices now have a member of staff who will deal with postal enquiries and supply copies of items for a set fee. This can prove to be quite expensive and you may be better off using the services of a reputable record agent or searcher in the area. See lists supplied by the record office, advertisements in ***Family Tree Magazine*** and ***Practical Family History*** or the list of the relevant Association of Genealogists & Record Agents for names.

Brief details of the principal repositories are all that can be given here. More information will be found either in the chapters or in the publications listed in the Chapter Bibliographies. Bear in mind that, with so much information now in microform, the records you wish to look at may be available in several repositories, not just the one that holds the original records, and you may be able to look at them via a computer-link. For example, many of the Scottish records can be consulted in London, and some Welsh records held in England can be read in Aberystwyth, or even on the Internet.

England and Wales

Family Records Centre: 1 Myddelton Street, Islington, London EC1R 1UW
This facility opened in 1997. The ground floor houses the civil registration indexes (see Chapter 8), formerly held by the Registrar General at St Catherine's House; the first floor has the census returns (see Chapter 9), and some other classes of records previously held at the Public Record Office branch in Chancery Lane. Both these buildings are now closed but you may still find them referred to in old editions of books mentioned in the chapter bibliographies.

Opening hours are Monday, Wednesday and Friday, 9.00am-5.00pm; Tuesday 10.00am-7.00pm; Thursday 9.00am-7.00pm and Saturday 9.30am-5.00pm.

Tel. numbers: Office for National Statistics (General Register Office) 0181 233 9233. Public Record Office 0181 392 5300.

No advance booking required for individuals; readers' tickets and proof of identity not required.

Public Record Office: Ruskin Avenue, Kew, Surrey TW9 4DU Tel. 0181 392 5261.
The PRO is described as 'the national archive for England and Wales'. Amongst records held here are those relating to the armed forces (including men from Scotland and Ireland), apprentices, divorces (from 1858), emigrants and immigrants and tax lists.

A series of Records Information leaflets, each one giving details of a class of records held, is currently available to personal callers at the PRO but cannot be requested by post. By mid-1998 it is anticipated that these leaflets will also be available at the PRO's web site on the Internet.

Opening hours are Monday, Wednesday, Friday, Saturday 9.30am-5pm; Tuesday 10am-7pm; Thursday 9.30am-7pm. No advance booking; a reader's ticket (obtainable on the spot – proof of identification needed) is available on the day.

Principal Registry of the Family Division: Wills and Letters of Administration from 1858 to present day; see Chapter 13. Indexes to these are being transferred during 1998 from Somerset House to the public search room in First Avenue House, High Holborn, London. Check (Tel. 0171 936 7000) before visiting.

'County' Record Offices: every county should have at least one Record Office or Archive, some of the larger ones have several. Documents described in Chapters 10 to 14 will normally be found here but check holdings before visiting. You will need to book (sometimes several weeks) in advance for most of them. Be aware that, due to financial constraints, some CROs are open only three days a week and very few are open on Saturdays. Most require a reader's ticket, generally available on your first visit. For addresses and telephone numbers see the Gibson Guide in the bibliography.

Libraries: many libraries, particularly those in cities and larger towns, maintain good local history collections. Apart from local material, an increasing number hold copies of the GRO Indexes on film or fiche and, in some cases, they hold the only complete county sets of census returns outside London – this is certainly the case in Yorkshire, where the main library in Leeds has microfilms of the 1841-1891 returns for the historic county. Most will hold copies of the 1881 Census Index and a few have full or partial sets of the post-1858 Wills Indexes (see Chapter 13).

British Library Newspaper Library: Colindale Avenue, London NW9 5HE.Tel. 0171 412 7353. Opening hours: Monday-Saturday 10.00am-4.45pm.

This library holds copies of most British and Irish newspapers and periodicals, principally since 1800, together with foreign and commonwealth ones. Some libraries may have more complete collections of their local papers.

National Library of Wales: Aberystwyth SY23 3BU Tel. 01970 632800. Holds many Welsh records, including microfiche copies of the GRO Indexes, microfilms of 1841-1891 census returns for Wales and originals or copies of many of the documents described in Chapters 10 to 14. Opening hours: Monday-Friday 9.30am-6.00pm. Restricted service on Saturday with opening hours 9.30am-5.00pm.

Society of Genealogists: 14 Charterhouse Buildings, Goswell Road, London EC1M 7BA Tel. 0171 251 8799. Members, and non-members on payment of a fee, have access to a superb library, including an extensive collection of printed and typed family histories. An outline guide ***Using the Library of the Society of Genealogists*** is available from the Society. Opening hours: Tuesday, Friday & Saturday 10.00am-6.00pm; Wednesday & Thursday 10.00am-8.00pm.

Scotland

Note: the two offices below are in adjacent buildings but are separate entities: do not confuse them!

General Register Office for Scotland: New Register House, Edinburgh EH1 3YT Tel. 0131 314 4433. Holds the indexes to, and the records of, births, marriages and deaths in Scotland, together with the census returns and the Old (pre-1855) Parish Registers. Advance booking is essential and a fee is payable to consult the indexes and records. Opening hours: Monday-Thursday 9.00am-4.30pm; Friday 9.00am-4.00pm.

An Internet service will be available by mid-1998 providing a fully searchable index to births/baptisms and banns/marriages from the OPRs 1553-1854 and to births, marriages and deaths from the civil registration indexes covering 1855-1897. The service will also provide an index to the 1891 census returns; the 1881 data should be made available later in 1998.

Scottish Record Office: General Register House, Edinburgh EH1 3YY. Tel. 0131 535 1314. A reader's ticket is required and will be issued on your first visit: no advance booking. The SRO holds many classes of records, including deposited Nonconformist registers and documents relating to probate, Kirk Sessions, land and house ownership, taxes, crime and punishment.

Scotland does not have CROs, the nearest equivalent being county libraries which are well stocked with local genealogical and historical books, microfilm copies of local material from the Edinburgh repositories, such as census returns and Old Parish Registers, and generally a collection of local newspapers either bound or on film. In Glasgow, the Mitchell Library is particularly good.

Scottish Genealogy Society: 15 Victoria Terrace, Edinburgh EH1 2JL has a wide range of material, including many Monumental Inscriptions recordings.

Ireland

The Republic of Ireland and Northern Ireland each have their own General Register Office and Public Record Office (see below); most of the other principal repositories are in Dublin, in the Republic. There are no county record offices in Ireland. The heritage and research centres, many of which developed from the Irish Genealogical Project initiated in the 1980s, are independent agencies providing a commercial genealogical research service.

General Register Office, Joyce House, 8-11 Lombard Street East, Dublin 2.
Tel. 1 (01 within Ireland) 711000. Opening hours: Monday-Friday 9.30am-12.30pm and 2.15pm-4.30pm.

General Register Office for Northern Ireland, Oxford House, 49-55 Chichester Street, Belfast BT1 4HL. Tel. 01232 252000. Opening Hours: Monday-Friday 9.30am-4.00pm.

A Reader's Ticket is required for most of the repositories below:

National Archives (amalgamation of the Public Record Office of Ireland and the State Paper Office), Bishop Street, Dublin 8. Tel. 1/01 (see GRO) 4783711. Opening hours: Monday-Friday 10.00am-5.00pm.

Public Record Office of Northern Ireland, 66 Balmoral Avenue, Belfast BT9 6NY. Tel. 01232 251318. Opening hours: Monday-Wednesday & Friday 9.15am-4.45pm; Thursday 9.15am-8.45pm.

National Library of Ireland, Kildare Street, Dublin 2. Tel. 1/01 (see GRO) 6030200. Opening hours: Monday-Wednesday 10.00am-9.00pm; Thursday-Friday 10.00am-5.00pm; Saturday 10.00am-1.00pm.

Registry of Deeds, King's Inns, Henrietta Street, Dublin 1.
Tel. 1/01 (see GRO) 6707500. Opening hours: Monday-Friday 10.00am-4.30pm.

Representative Church Body Library, Braemor Park, Rathgar, Dublin 14.
Tel. 1/01 (see GRO) 4923979. Opening hours: Monday-Friday 9.00am-1.00pm & 1.45pm-5.00pm.

Channel Islands

Civil Registration

Jersey
Superintendent Registrar, States Office, 10 Royal Square, St Helier, Jersey.

Guernsey and the other Islands
Registrar General, The Greffe, Royal Court House, St Peter Port, Guernsey GY1 2PD.

Isle of Man

Civil Registry, Deemster's Walk, Bucks Road, Douglas, Isle of Man IM1 3AR.
Opening hours: Monday-Friday 9am-1pm and 2.15pm-4.30pm.

Manx Museum Library, Kingswood Grove, Douglas, Isle of Man.

Family History Centres (FHC)

The Church of Jesus Christ of Latter-day Saints (Mormons) can be found throughout the world. Their FHCs are genealogical libraries attached to some, but by no means all, of their churches. For a small fee it is possible to order for study any record which the LDS church has filmed (including census returns and many parish registers/bishops' transcripts); some centres hold filmed copies of the various British civil registration indexes and all have the IGI and 1881 census indexes (see Chapter 7). A complete list of FHCs in the United Kingdom can be obtained from The Genealogical Society of Utah, 185 Penns Lane, Sutton Coldfield, West Midlands B76 1JU (don't forget to send an s.a.e.); there are also lists in ***The Family Historian's Enquire Within*** and ***Tracing Your Family Tree*** (see Bibliography, Chapter 3) and ***An Introduction to Civil Registration*** (see Chapter 8). The name, incidentally, was changed from Family History Library to Family History Centre to avoid confusion because people went there, expecting to find a library of books, and found that almost everything was available in microform, not in book form.

You do not have to be a member of the LDS church to use these Family History Centres, which are freely open to all; no visitor need fear that any attempt to convert them will be made. FHCs are staffed by volunteers (many of whom are members of the local family history society rather than LDS members) and have restricted opening hours, which should be ascertained when planning a visit.

Bear in mind that the Genealogical Society of Utah's Family History Library at 35 North West Temple, Salt Lake City, Utah 84150, USA contains the largest genealogical library in the world and access to this collection is obtainable through any FHC. The material to be found within a local FHC is only a fraction of that held in Salt Lake City. For some counties (like Yorkshire), where records are spread between a number of record offices in one county, it can actually be easier for some researchers to work in Utah (with the records under one roof) than in England!

Bibliography

Basic Facts about Archives, Susan Lumas. FFHS, 1997.

Record Repositories in Great Britain, 10th edition. HMSO, 1997.

The Genealogical Services Directory, Robert Blatchford and Geoffrey Heslop. GR Specialist Information Services, 1998.

Basic Facts about Using the Family Records Centre, Audrey Collins. FFHS, 1997.

Never Been Here Before? (Family Records Centre), Jane Cox & Stella Colwell. PRO Publications, 1997.

New to Kew? (Public Record Office), Jane Cox. PRO Publications, 1997.

Tracing Your Ancestors in the Public Record Office, 4th edition, Amanda Bevan & Andrea Duncan. London, HMSO, 1990.

Basic Facts about Using Record Offices for Family Historians, Tom Wood. FFHS, 1996.

Record Offices: How to Find Them, 8th edition, Jeremy Gibson & Pamela Peskett. FFHS, 1998.

Basic Facts about Family History Research in Lancashire, Rita Hirst. FFHS, 1997.

Basic Facts about Family History Research in Yorkshire, Pauline Litton. FFHS, 1995.

Welsh Family History: A guide to research, 2nd edition, ed. John & Sheila Rowlands et al. FFHS, 1998.

Researching Family History in Wales [repositories + main holdings], Jean Istance & E.E.Cann. FFHS, 1996.

Basic Facts about Family History Research in Glamorgan, Rosemary Davies. FFHS, 1998.

Scottish Roots, revised edition, Alwyn James. Saltire Society, 1995.

Tracing Your Scottish Ancestry, Kathleen B. Cory. Polygon, 1990.

Tracing Your Ancestors in the Scottish Record Office, Cecil Sinclair. Edinburgh, HMSO, 1990.

Exploring Scottish History, a Directory of Resource Centres for Local and National History in Scotland, ed. Michael Cox. Scottish Local History Forum, 1992.

Introduction to Irish Research, 2nd edition (revised), Bill Davis. FFHS, 1998.

Tracing your Irish Ancestors, John Grenham. Gill & Macmillan, 1992.

Tracing Irish Ancestors, Máire MacConghail and Paul Gorry. Harper-Collins, Collins Pocket Reference, 1997.

Irish Genealogy: A Record Finder, ed. Donal F. Begley. Heraldic Artists Ltd, 1981

Family History in Jersey, Marie-Louise Backhurst. Channel Islands FHS, 1992. (second edition due 1998)

Manx Family Tree: A Beginners' Guide to Records in the Isle of Man, Janet Narasimham. Isle of Man, reprinted 1994.

CHAPTER SIX

Abbreviations and Codes

Abbreviations

Family historians are sometimes accused of using a language of their own because we tend to use shortened forms of many words to save space on pedigree charts, in our notes and in books, and because we use initials for many of the record repositories and organisations concerned with our hobby. The lists which follow on pages 34-36 include most of those abbreviations which are in common use; very obvious ones, like bap., mar. and bur. for baptism, marriage and burial, have been omitted. Some letters or groups of letters have more than one meaning; the context should enable you to work out which one is meant. Some of them are in/from Latin and are often used in printed pedigrees (see Chapter 4) and in early Parish Registers (see Chapter 10). Do not be put off by this; with this key you should be able to cope. Bear in mind that most abbreviations are of two, three or more letters. Using a single letter (apart from certain capital letters) can be very risky: **b** (most commonly used for born) has also been used for baptised, before, or buried. Be consistent in the use of abbreviations and keep a key with your own records.

Codes

The **Chapman County Codes**, listed on pages 37-38, are three-letter abbreviations for the counties of the British Isles. The system was devised in the late 1970s and is still widely used for family history purposes. You will find them in most genealogical publications, including this one, and in the majority of indexes, although the 1881 census index (see Chapter 7) does sometimes stray from them.

The General Register Office Indexes, listed on page 39, could equally be included in Chapters 7 or 8 but they contain an important 'code' element in that the Roman or Arabic numeral given for each entry enables you to ascertain the county in which it was registered. This can be essential if you are faced with an unfamiliar Registration District. For example, you will not find the RD of Thingoe in a gazetteer or on a map but the code 4a will tell you that it is in Essex or Suffolk and further enquiry will reveal that it covers the area around Bury St Edmunds. Similarly, many family historians have fallen into the trap of believing that the RD of West Derby refers to part of the county of Derbyshire whereas, in fact, it is a suburb of Liverpool in Lancashire, and its 8b code (Derbyshire would be 7b) helps you to realise this.

Abbreviations commonly used for Printed Pedigrees and Records

English

admon.	Letters of Administration
ag. lab.	agricultural labourer
B	Banns
bach.	bachelor
Bd	Bond
bn	born
botp	both of this parish
Bp	Bishop
C	Century (as in C18)
cent.	century
cod.	codicil
Ct.	Court
div.	divorce
educ.	educated at
exec.	executor/executrix
fol.	folio
FS	Female Servant (1841 census)
FWK	framework knitter
ill./illeg.	illegitimate
inf.	infant
inv.	inventory
kia	killed in action
Lic.	licence
MS	Male Servant (1841 census)
obit.	died **or** obituary
otp	of this parish
prob.	probate
sp.	spinster
wcop	with consent of parents
wdr.	widower
wdw.	widow
wf.	wife
wid.	widow **or** widower
wit.	witness

Latin

aet. [45]	aged [45]
al[ia]s	also/otherwise known as
cae[lebs].	unmarried i.e. bach. **or** wdr.
c[irca]	about/approximately
conj.	married
de	of
d[itt]o	as previous statement
dsp.	died without issue
e[odem] d[ie]	the same day
eius	his
et al	and others
f[ilius]/f[ilia]	son or daughter
gem[elli]	twins
hic jacet	here lies (on MI)
IPM	Inquisition Post Mortem
mat.	maternal/mother
matr.	married
nat[us]	born
nup.	recently
nupt.	married
ob[it].	died
opp[idum]	town
osp	died without issue
pat.	paternal/father
praedict.	as previously stated
rec[to]	reverse side of folio
rel[icta]	widow
sep.	bur.
sic	thus (as written)
T[estamenta]	Will
temp.	in the time of
ux[or]	wife
verso	front page of folio

Latin Names and Numbers

Most Christian names are very similar in their Latin and English forms.

Common ones which might cause problems are:

Anna which can mean Anne, Hannah or Nancy
Carolus which is Charles
Gulielmus which is William
Jacobus which can mean James or Jacob
Radulphus which is Ralph
Xpofer which is Christopher

Roman numerals are often used before 1733 for dates in Parish Registers (and for sums of money in Wills and Inventories). Some incumbents and clerks wrote out the Latin words, or sometimes shortened forms of them. Three common formats for the days of the month are given below.

1st	i	primo
2nd	ii	secundo
3rd	iii	tertio
4th	iiii/iv	quarto
5th	v	quinto
6th	vi	sexto
7th	vii	septimo
8th	viii	octavo
9th	ix	nono
10th	x	decimo
11th	xi	undecimo
12th	xii	duodecimo
13th	xiii	decimo tertio
14th	xiv	decimo quarto
15th	xv	decimo quinto
16th	xvi	decimo sexto
17th	xvii	decimo septimo
18th	xviii	decimo octavo
19th	xix	decimo nono
20th	xx	vicesimo
21st	xxi	vicesimo primo
22nd	xxii	vic. secundo
23rd	xxiii	vic. tertio
24th	xxiv	vic. quarto
25th	xxv	vic. quinto
26th	xxvi	vic. sexto
27th	xxvii	vic. septimo
28th	xxviii	vic. octavo
29th	xxix	vicesimo nono
30th	xxx	tricesimo
31st	xxxi	trecesimo primo

The Latin names for the months are very similar to their English equivalents and should cause you no problems.

A word of warning: as detailed in Chapter 10, before 1752 the year in England and Wales began on 25th March. September, October, November and December were the seventh to tenth months of that calendar, often abbreviated to 7ber, 8ber, 9ber, 10ber. Remember this and do not make the mistake of interpreting them as July-October, the seventh to tenth months of the modern (post-1751) calendar.

Commonly Used Abbreviations

BMD	Births, Marriages, Deaths	**ONS (2)**	One-Name Study
BT	Bishop's Transcript	**OPR**	Old Parish Register (Scotland)
CMB	Christenings, Marriages, Burials	**OS**	Ordnance Survey
CRO	County Record Office	**PCC (1)**	Prerogative Court of Canterbury
CWGC	Commonwealth War Graves Commission	**PCC (2)**	Parochial Church Council
		PCY	Prerogative Court of York
DNB	Dictionary of National Biography	**PLU**	Poor Law Union
DRO	Diocesan Record Office	**PPR**	Principal Probate Registry
EIC	East India Company	**PR**	Parish Register
GRO	General Register Office	**PRO**	Public Record Office
HMSO	Her Majesty's Stationery Office	**QS**	Quarter Sessions
IGI	International Genealogical Index	**RD**	Registration District
MI	Monumental/Memorial Inscription	**RO**	Record Office
NBI	National Burials Index	**SLC**	Salt Lake City
NLW	National Library of Wales	**VCH**	Victoria County History
NRA	National Register of Archives	**WO**	War Office
ONS (1)	Office for National Statistics		

Note: some Record Offices locally may be referred to by initials which can easily be confused with national offices listed above – bear in mind that, for example, GRO may be used in Wales for Glamorgan Record Office and CRO in the southwest for Cornwall Record Office, or in the northwest for Cumbria Record Office!

Organisations

AFHSW	Association of FHSs in Wales
AGRA	Association of Genealogists & Record Agents
APGI	Association of Professional Genealogists in Ireland
AUGRA	Association of Ulster Genealogists and Record Agents
BALH	British Association for Local History
BIG R	British Isles Genealogical Register
FFHS	Federation of Family History Societies
FHS	Family History Society
FTM	Family Tree Magazine
GOONS	Guild of One-Name Studies
GRD	Genealogical Research Directory
GSU	Genealogical Society of Utah
IHGS	Institute of Heraldic & Genealogical Studies
LDS	(Church of Jesus Christ of) Latter-day Saints [Mormons]
NGD	National Genealogical Directory
SAFHS	Scottish Association of FHSs
SAGRA	Scottish Association of Genealogists and Record Agents
SGS	Scottish Genealogy Society
SoG	Society of Genealogists

Chapman County Codes

Before 1974: 1975 for Scotland

England (ENG)

BDF	Bedfordshire
BRK	Berkshire
BKM	Buckinghamshire
CAM	Cambridgeshire
CHS	Cheshire
CON	Cornwall
CUL	Cumberland
DBY	Derbyshire
DEV	Devonshire
DOR	Dorset
DUR	Durham
ESS	Essex
GLS	Gloucestershire
HAM	Hampshire
HEF	Herefordshire
HRT	Hertfordshire
HUN	Huntingdonshire
KEN	Kent
LAN	Lancashire
LEI	Leicestershire
LIN	Lincolnshire
LND	London
MDX	Middlesex
NBL	Northumberland
NFK	Norfolk
NTH	Northamptonshire
NTT	Nottinghamshire
OXF	Oxfordshire
RUT	Rutland
SAL	Shropshire
SFK	Suffolk
SOM	Somerset
SRY	Surrey
SSX	Sussex
STS	Staffordshire
WAR	Warwickshire
WES	Westmorland
WIL	Wiltshire
WOR	Worcestershire
YKS	Yorkshire
ERY	Yks East Riding
NRY	Yks North Riding
WRY	Yks West Riding
IOW	Isle of Wight
IOM	Isle of Man

Wales (WLS):

AGY	Anglesey
BRE	Brecknockshire
CAE	Caernarvonshire
CGN	Cardiganshire
CMN	Carmarthenshire
DEN	Denbighshire
FLN	Flintshire
GLA	Glamorgan
MER	Merionethshire
MGY	Montgomeryshire
MON	Monmouthshire
PEM	Pembrokeshire
RAD	Radnorshire

Scotland (SCT):

ABD	Aberdeenshire
ANS	Angus
ARL	Argyllshire
AYR	Ayrshire
BAN	Banffshire
BEW	Berwickshire
BUT	Bute
CAI	Caithness
CLK	Clackmannanshire
DFS	Dumfriesshire
DNB	Dunbartonshire
ELN	East Lothian
FIF	Fife
	Forfarshire (see Angus)
INV	Inverness-shire
KCD	Kincardineshire
KKD	Kirkcudbrightshire
KRS	Kinross-shire
LKS	Lanarkshire
MLN	Midlothian
MOR	Moray
NAI	Nairnshire
OKI	Orkney Isles

PEE	Peebles-shire
PER	Perthshire
RFW	Renfrewshire
ROC	Ross & Cromarty
ROX	Roxburghshire
SEL	Selkirkshire
SHI	Shetland Isles
STI	Stirlingshire
SUT	Sutherland
WIG	Wigtownshire
WLN	West Lothian

Channel Islands (CHI):

ALD	Alderney
GSY	Guernsey
JSY	Jersey
SRK	Sark

Ireland (IRL):

CAR	Carlow
CAV	Cavan
CLA	Clare
COR	Cork
DON	Donegal
DUB	Dublin
GAL	Galway
KER	Kerry
KID	Kildare
KIK	Kilkenny
	Kings (see Offaly)
LET	Leitrim
LEX	Leix (Queens)
LIM	Limerick
LOG	Longford
LOU	Louth
MAY	Mayo
MEA	Meath
MOG	Monaghan
OFF	Offaly (Kings)
	Queens (see Leix)
ROS	Roscommon
SLI	Sligo
TIP	Tipperary
WAT	Waterford
WEM	Westmeath
WEX	Wexford
WIC	Wicklow

N. Ireland (NIR):

ANT	Antrim
ARM	Armagh
DOW	Down
FER	Fermanagh
LDY	Londonderry
TYR	Tyrone

England (ENG) after 1974:

AVN	Avon
CLV	Cleveland
CMA	Cumbria
GTM	Greater Manchester
HWR	Hereford & Worcester
HUM	Humberside
MSY	Merseyside
SXE	East Sussex
SXW	West Sussex
TWR	Tyne & Wear
WMD	West Midlands
NYK	North Yorkshire
SYK	South Yorkshire
WYK	West Yorkshire

Wales (WLS): after 1974

CWD	Clwyd
DFD	Dyfed
GNT	Gwent
GWN	Gwynedd
MGM	Mid Glamorgan
POW	Powys
SGM	South Glamorgan
WGM	West Glamorgan

Scotland (SCT): after 1975

BOR	Borders
CEN	Central Region
DGY	Dumfries & Galloway
GMP	Grampian
HLD	Highland
LTN	Lothian
STD	Strathclyde
TAY	Tayside
WIS	Western Isles

After the 1974 local government re-organisation most counties retained their historic names (and therefore the same three letter codes). The new counties which came into being at that time are listed on page 38. Some of these recent creations were in their turn abolished in further re-organisation in the mid-1990s but their codes remain in the list for reference purposes.

Codes employed in the General Register Office Indexes

Anglesey	XXVII 11b
Bedfordshire	VI 3b
Berkshire	VI 2c
Brecknockshire	XXVI 11b
Buckinghamshire	VI 3a
Caernarvonshire	XXVII 11b
Cambridgeshire	XIV 3b
Cardiganshire	XXVII 11b
Carmarthenshire	XXVI 11b
Cheshire	XIX 8a
Cornwall	IX 5c
Cumberland	XXV 10b
Denbighshire	XXVII 11b
Derbyshire	XIX 7b
Devonshire	IX, X 5b
Dorset	VIII 5a
Durham	XXIV 10a
Essex	XII 4a
Flintshire	XIX, XXVII 11b
Glamorganshire	XXVI 11a
Gloucestershire	XI, XVIII 6a
Hampshire	VII, VIII, 2b, 2c
Herefordshire	XXVI 6a
Hertfordshire	VI 3a
Huntingdonshire	XIV 3b
Kent	V, 1d,2a
Lancashire	XX, XXI, XXV, 8b,8c 8d,8e
Leicestershire	XV 7a

Lincolnshire	XIV 7a
London (with suburbs)	I, II, III, IV, 1a, 1b, 1c, 1d
Merionethshire	XXVII 11b
Middlesex	I, II, III 1a, 1b,1c,3a
Monmouthshire	XXVI 11a
Montgomeryshire	XXVII 11b
Norfolk	XIII 4b
Northamptonshire	XV 3b
Northumberland	XXV 10b
Nottinghamshire	XV 7b
Oxfordshire	XIV 3a
Pembrokeshire	XXVI 11a
Radnorshire	XXVI 11b
Rutland	XV 7a
Shropshire	XXVI, XVIII 6a
Somerset	X, XI 5c
Staffordshire	XVI,XVII,XVIII 6b
Suffolk	XVI, XII, XIII, 3b, 4a
Surrey	IV, 1d, 2a
Sussex	VII 2b
Warwickshire	XI, XVI, XVIII 6b, 6c, 6d
Westmorland	XXV 10b
Wiltshire	VIII 5a
Worcestershire	XVIII, 6b, 6c
Yorkshire	XXI, XXII, XXIII,XXIV, 9a, 9b, 9c, 9d

Note: Roman numerals were used from 1837-1851.
Arabic numerals were used from 1852 onwards.

Bibliography

Latin for Local History: an Introduction, Eileen A.Gooder. Longman, 1978.
A Latin Glossary for Family & Local Historians, Janet Morris. FFHS, 1989.
Dates & Calendars for the Genealogist, Clifford Webb. SoG, 1989.

CHAPTER SEVEN

Indexes

Throughout this book you will find reference to all kinds of indexes. Before the explosion of interest in family history in the 1970s there were very few indexes which were helpful to those researching their ancestors; now there are thousands of them. Smaller ones may contain only a few hundred names, larger ones more than 187 million. Don't forget the proverb 'the best things come in small parcels' – a specialised index with very few entries may hold the vital piece of information you need, the largest one may not include the very ancestor you want.

Indexes can come in many forms – as a book, a card index, on microfiche, microfilm, as a database, on CD-ROM or on the Internet – and cover almost any subject or type of record. They range from the major ones described in Chapter 4 and below to more specialised ones covering, for example, *Seamen at the Battle of Trafalgar*, *Multiple Births* and *Tobacco Pipe Makers*.

Always ask in any record repository, or when you join a family history society, what indexes they hold or are aware of. Read the books recommended in the bibliography to this chapter to find details of indexes being compiled by societies and individuals. Many, particularly for census returns (see Chapter 9) and marriage indexes, are available for purchase; others are held by societies or individuals who offer a search service in return for a small fee.

An index is most commonly an alphabetically sorted list, usually by surname or placename, but do not take it for granted that all indexes are compiled using precisely the same format.

The International Genealogical Index, in common with some marriage indexes, groups all variants of a surname together in one sequence so that under Pelling you will find listed all entries for Peeling/Peling/Pellan/Pellen/Pellin/Pelling/Pellinge/Pellings/Pellyng (see page 42). However, be careful as the system does not always use the groupings you would expect, so where Whittington and Wittington both come under the former, Whenham and Wenham (see page 61) are listed separately.

The 1881 Census Index, the GRO Indexes (see Chapters 6 and 8) and the majority of other indexes list names in strict alphabetical order so you will need to check every possible variant individually. Whitaker and Whittaker are separated by White/Whitehead/Whitehurst etc. and may be several fiche apart.

Some so-called indexes are, in fact, calendars and these list names only by their first letter (occasionally by the first two or three letters) so that Penfold may come before Pelling, and both before Passiful. It is always worth taking a few minutes to read the introduction or to work out precisely which system has been used for the particular index at which you are looking.

Two of the indexes mentioned currently have such a high profile in family history research that they merit further explanation. You will want to consult these early in your research as they may well offer you a 'short cut' to locating earlier generations of your ancestors.

International Genealogical Index and FamilySearch

The IGI, compiled by computer and first produced in 1973 as the Computer File Index (a name which you may find in some older books), has revolutionised genealogical research. Books published before the IGI was generally available suggest that Civil Registration (see Chapter 8) is the first source to research. Since, however, registration certificates have to be purchased it is prudent to consult the IGI first but read the rest of this section before you do!

The IGI is produced by the LDS Church to help its members in their religious work. That is its primary purpose but its contents are available to anyone, including non-members of the Church, who wishes to use it for family history research. It is an on-going project, with new entries being added all the time. The number of entries is staggering; the 1973 edition included 20 million names worldwide, the 1998 contains 284 million names (of which more than 72 million are in the British Isles fiche). You would be well advised to make sure that you look at a recent edition.

It includes principally baptism and marriage entries, mostly covering the period before 1875. Burials are not usually included. The number of baptisms is much greater than the number of marriage entries. Marriages are indexed under the names of both bride and bridegroom. The index is on microfiche, *i.e.* small sheets of microfilm about four inches by six inches, each containing about 16,000 names. The fiche is inserted into a reader, which is very simple to operate. Names in the British Isles fiche are arranged by county, alphabetically by surname, then by given name, and then chronologically. The latest technological development is the transfer of the index onto compact disc/CD ROM, as part of FamilySearch (see below); with this system, countrywide (instead of county) searches are possible.

The IGI is widely available. Complete sets are held at the LDS Church's Family History Centres worldwide. Full sets for the UK and sometimes other areas are also held by many organisations, including the Society of Genealogists, some of the larger family history societies, and many reference libraries. County Record Offices and Family History Societies may hold the index for their county (and possibly neighbouring ones), as do some individuals. It is possible to obtain print-outs from the IGI, listing, for example, all the Pelling entries in Sussex, so that you can study them at your leisure: (see page 42). The Society of Genealogists offers this service, as do a number of other organisations who advertise in genealogical publications such as ***Family Tree Magazine*** (available from newsagents and bookshops).

PELLING, MARY

COUNTRY: ENGLAND — COUNTY: SUSSEX — AS OF MAR 1992 — PAGE 17,799

NAME: PELLING, MARY — M=MALE F=FEMALE H=HUSBAND W=WIFE

NAME	FATHER / MOTHER OR SPOUSE OR RELATIVE		TYPE	EVENT DATE	TOWN, PARISH	B	E	S	SOURCE: BATCH/FILM NO	SOURCE: SERIAL/SHEET
PELLING, MARY	JOHN HOAD	W	M	14FEB1731	LAUGHTON			16MAY1956SL	0457049	1317
PELLING, MARY @	SPOUSE: WILLIAM TURNER/	F	B	ABT. 1734	OF ISFIELD	11DEC1[illegible]LG	28JAN1955LG	PRE-1970	0447881	FILM
PELLING, MARY	JAMES BISHOP	W	M	20APR1740	NEWTIMBER			17SEP1981SL	M070651	0361
PELLING, MARY @	JOHN PELLING/SARAH	F	B	25JAN1746	BRIGHTON	26APR1961AZ	17MAY1961AZ	PRE-1970	0451122	FILM
PELLING, MARY	WILLM PELLING/ELIZ	F	C	13APR1746	HORSTED KEYNES	06JUL1978OK	29SEP1978OK	13OCT1978OK	C070651	1728
PELLEN, MRS. MARY @	SPOUSE: JOHN PELLEN/	F	B	ABT. 1754	OF NEWTIMBER	26APR1961AZ	17MAY1961AZ	PRE-1970	045[illegible]122	FILM
PELLING, MRS. MARY @	SPOUSE: THOMAS PELLING/	F	B	ABT. 1759	OF BRIGHTON	26APR1961AZ	17MAY1961AZ	PRE-1970	0451122	FILM
PELLING, MARY	WILLIAM TURNER	W	M	26SEP1765	ISFIELD			18MAY1955SL	[illegible]	0216
PEALING, MARY	THOMAS PEALING/ANN	F	C	13APR1766	PIDDINGHOE	16SEP1989SG	10NOV1989SG	16NOV1989SG	K148221	0745
PELLING, MARY	THOS PELLING/MARY	F	C	08FEB1767	HORSTED KEYNES	07JUL1978OK	30SEP1978OK	18OCT1978OK	C070651	[illegible]209
PELLING, MARY @	PELLING/	F	B	ABT. 1770	OF BRIGHTON	26APR1961AZ	17MAY1961AZ	PRE-1970	0451122	FILM
PELLING, MARY @	THOMAS PELLING/MARY GATLAND	F	B	1773	BRIGHTON	26APR1961AZ	17MAY1961AZ	PRE-1970	0451122	FILM
PELLEN, MARY	JOHN PELLEN/ELIZABETH	F	C	03APR1774	NEWTIMBER	15DEC1978WA	31JAN1979WA	31MAR1979WA	C070861	0441
PELLEN, MARY @	JOHN PELLEN/MARY	F	B	19MAR1782	NEWTIMBER	26APR1961AZ	17MAY1961AZ	PRE-1970	0451122	FILM
PELLING, MARY @	THOMAS PELLING/REBECCA	F	B	07DEC1793	BRIGHTON	26APR1961AZ	17MAY1961AZ	PRE-1970	0451122	FILM
PELLING, MARY	HENRY PELLING/MARY	F	C	04NOV1798	BRIGHTON, NORTH STREET-COUNTESS OF HUNTINGDONS OR DISSENTING PROTESTANT	24JUN1978AL	30AUG1978AL	25OCT1978AL	C075991	0305
PELLING, MARY	JEREMIAH SIMMONDS	W	M	05SEP1804	LEWES, ST. ANNE			04DEC1988LA	86[illegible]0532	[illegible]20
PELLEN, MARY	JAMES PELLEN/FRANCES	F	C	22DEC1805	BARLAVINGTON	19JUN1980PV	24SEP1980PV	25OCT1980PV	C070082	0096
PELLEN, MARY	/SARAH PELLEN	F	C	28FEB1813	FRANT	27APR1988JR	20MAY1988JR		K148461	4616
PELLING, MARY	JAMES PELLING/ANN	F	C	18JUL1824	LEWES, OLD CHAPEL IN THE CLIFF-COUNTESS OF HUNTINGDONS	18JUL1978PV	14SEP1978PV	03NOV1978PV	C076191	0455
PELLEN, MARY	THOMAS HOADE	W	M	17MAY1829	WISTON			30MAR1981SL	M071311	0283
PELLING, MARY @	RELATIVE: WILLIE S. DANIELS/	F	B	1856		27MAR1917SL	PRE-1970	PRE-1970	0183469	FILM
PELLEN, MARY	JOHN PELLEN/SARAH	F	C	30MAR1856	NEWTIMBER	15DEC1978WA	01FEB1979WA	31MAR1979WA	C070861	0835
PELLING, MARY	JOHN CORPS	W	M	10JAN1861	WEST HOATHLY			01NOV1980OG	M070631	0582
PELLING, MARY	/SARAH ANN PELLING	F	C	29SEP1869	FRANT	29SEP1989SG	22NOV1989SG		K148463	3263
PELLING, MARY	JACOB MUGGRIDGE	W	M	22OCT1872	RUDGWICK			23MAR1981SL	M070971	1858
PELLING, MARY ANN @	PELLING/MARY PELLING	F	B	03FEB1792	BRIGHTON	26APR1961AZ	17MAY1961AZ	PRE-1970	0451122	FILM
PELLEN, MARY ANN	THOMAS PELLEN/PHILADELPHIA	F	C	13NOV1808	WEST HOATHLY	05OCT1978MT	10NOV1978MT	06FEB1979MT	C070631	3159
PELLEN, MARY ANN	JOSEPH PELLEN/ELIZABETH	F	C	22FEB1834	SLINFOLD	CHILD	CHILD	21FEB1979MT	C071091	3738
PELLING, MARY ANN	JOHN BOWLES	W	M	02MAR1834	BRIGHTON, SAINT NICHOLAS			28JUL1989JR	M147935	2397
PELLING, MARY ANN	JAMES PELLING/HARRIETT	F	C	18NOV1866	RUDGWICK	07NOV1978IF	09FEB1979IF	27FEB1979IF	C070971	6456
PELLING, MARY ANN ‡	WILLIAM LUCK	W	M	03OCT1868	FRANT			23MAR1988DV	M148462	0605
PELLING, MARY ANNE	EDMUND HILLS	W	M	03JAN1829	WEST HOATHLY			31OCT1930OG	M070631	0393
PELLING, MARY ANNE	THOMAS PELLING/SARAH	F	C	31AUG1845	FRANT	27SEP1989SG	18NOV1989SG	28NOV1989SG	K148463	1205
PELLING, MARY ANNE	JOHN COOPER	W	M	30MAR1872	NEWTIMBER			17SEP1981SL	M070861	0266
PELLING, MARY JANE	JOSEPH PELLING/KEZIA	F	C	08MAR1863	SLINFOLD	20OCT1978MT	10JAN1979MT	21FEB1979MT	C071091	4379
PELLING, MARY JANE	GEORGE PELLING/SUSAN	F	C	01APR1866	SHIPLEY	18NOV1978LA	02FEB1979LA	15FEB1979LA	C071041	6535
PELLING, MARY STRUTFIELD	JOHN PELLING/ELIZABETH	F	C	24FEB1811	CHIDDINGLY	06APR1979PV	17MAY1979PV	12JUL1979PV	C099681	2826
PELLING, MARYANNE		F	C	29MAR1840	WEST HOATHLY	05OCT1978MT	15NOV1978MT	08FEB1979MT	C070631	4167
PELLING, MELLIE @	WILLIAM PELLING/CHARLOTTE; RELATIVE: WILLIAM S. DANIELS/	F	B	07NOV1866	PIECOMBE	19JUN1928LG	PRE-1970	PRE-1970	0177905	FILM
PELLEN, MERCY	HENRY PELLEN/FRANCES ELIZABETH	F	C	25SEP1864	NEWTIMBER	15DEC1978WA	01FEB1979WA	31MAR1979WA	C070861	0891
PELLING, MICHAEL	JOSE PELLING/HANNAH	M	C	06OCT1816	RUDGWICK	03NOV1978IF	27FEB1979IF	09MAR1979IF	C070971	6532
PELLING, MICHAEL	ANN BURFOOT	H	M	17MAR1846	HORSHAM			15FEB1980PV	M070641	3924
PELLING, MICHAEL	WILLIAM PELLING/ANNE	M	C	21JAN1867	SOUTHWATER	02DEC1978AL	28FEB1979AL	04APR1979AL	C071141	0447
PELLINGE, MICHAELL	RIC. PELLINGE/	M	C	16MAR1552	HURSTMONCEUX	02SEP1987OG	24NOV1987OG	03DEC1987OG	8707030	[illegible]17
PELLING, MIMA	WILLIAM SIMMONS	W	M	10OCT1796	MARESFIELD			07MAY1971SW	7010316	[illegible]88
PELLING, MIMA	WILLIAM SIMMONS	W	M	10OCT1796	MARESFIELD			05APR1928SL	A184618	3364
PELLING, MINA @	RELATIVE: CAROLINE S. BALL/	F	M	10OCT1796	MARESFIELD	05MAY1924SL	PRE-1970	PRE-1970	0183509	FILM
PELLING, NAOMI	JAMES PELLING/NAOMI	F	C	15APR1860	ALFRISTON	23FEB1988SE	29MAR1988SE	05APR1988SE	8721233	[illegible]5
PELLING, NOAH	JOSE PELLING/HANNAH	M	C	10OCT1810	RUDGWICK	02NOV1978IF	27FEB1979IF	09MAR1979IF	C070971	6224
PELLING, NOAH	ANN PARSONS	H	M	21MAY1834	RUDGWICK			23MAR1981SL	M070971	1546

Δ= ENTRY ALTERED FROM SOURCE; ‡,@,>=RELATIVES NAMED IN SOURCE. SEE "SYMBOLS" IN INSTRUCTIONS.

A = ADULT CHRISTENING B = BIRTH C = CHRISTENING D = DEATH OR BURIAL ALL OTHERS = MISCELLANEOUS
F = BIRTH OR CHRISTENING OF FIRST KNOWN CHILD M = MARRIAGE N= CENSUS W = WILL

Sample Page from the International Genealogical Index

It must be emphasised that the IGI is an index and, like any other index, contains errors and omissions. It has been prepared not only from printed sources and original records but also from entries submitted by members of the Church and they, like all of us, can be expected to have made some mistakes. It does not have complete coverage of the records for any county. An important point to keep in mind is that only an estimated 45% of all parish register entries are included and, even when there are entries for a parish, it does not mean that all the registers have been indexed. All indexes are the tools of genealogical research but their contents should not be accepted as a substitute for primary source information. Once an entry is found in any index it should be checked by reference to the original record.

FamilySearch, a series of computer programs and files which operates on read-only compact discs, is the most recent development in the field of family history research. It incorporates the IGI, Ancestral File (a pedigree-linked file of millions of names) and the Family History Library Catalog (a listing with description and library call numbers for the library collection of the Family History Library in Salt Lake City). Again, FHCs, the Society of Genealogists and an increasing number of libraries and larger FHSs hold copies.

A word of warning – some people place too much reliance on entries in the IGI and compile entire family trees from this source alone, without confirming details from the original records. This is a dangerous practice. Many entries refer to children who were baptised but died before the age of seven and a surprising number of these appear as parents and grandparents on family trees which have been put together after a short period in front of a microfiche reader.

1881 Census Index

This is the culmination of a project undertaken between 1988 and 1996 to index the complete 1881 census for the British Isles (excluding Ireland). The results were produced on microfiche. Indexes are currently available for each county in England, Wales, the Isle of Man, and the Channel Islands, providing coverage of all those resident in these places on 3 April 1881. A National Index on CD ROM is expected in 1998. Meanwhile, all sections may be seen at the LDS Library in Salt Lake City, at their FHCs throughout the world, at the Family Records Centre and the Society of Genealogists in London, and at some other major libraries. Many record offices, libraries and FHSs hold the sections for their own counties. The Index for Scotland may be seen at New Register House, at FHCs and on the Internet from late 1998.

The present index is in seven separate sections, with a different coloured strip at the top of each fiche. These are:

1. Surname Index (pink strip)
2. Birthplace Index (green)
3. Census Place Index (orange)
4. As Enumerated (yellow)
5. List of Vessels or Ships (brown) – not for all counties
6. List of Institutions (brown)
7. Miscellaneous Notes (brown).

The first three sections contain the same information, differently presented, and which of them you look at first depends on what you know and what you hope to find. The Surname Index gives Surname, Forename, Age, Sex, Relationship to Head of Household, Marital Condition, Census Place (i.e. where resident on census night 1881), Occupation, Name of Head of Household, Where Born and References (to enable you to locate the entry either on the As Enumerated Fiche or on a microfilm of the census returns). The Birthplace Index gives Surname with Where Born (alphabetically) and follows this with all the information as in the Surname Index, except that Occupation is omitted. The Census Place Index has Surname, followed by Census Place (alphabetically), and then by the other information (except Occupation).

Trying to find Alexander Pelling in 1881, the Surname Index for Surrey (his county of birth) was consulted but no trace of him was found. He does not appear on the 1881 census index in any of the Home Counties. However, other members of his family were in the various indexes. The Birthplace Index gave all the Pellings born in Ewhurst (where he was born) and Dorking (where he later married) and where they were living in 1881; the Census Place Index provided the Pellings living in Ewhurst and Dorking in 1881 and where they were born. By examining all three indexes it was possible to 're-unite' families whose children had left home and build up a picture of the migration of several groups from Sussex to Surrey and within the counties.

Look at the Surname Index fiche print-out on page 45. George Pelling, shown there aged 28, is a son of Michael and an elder brother of Alexander, direct ancestors as shown on the Line Pedigree on page 22. Study the As Enumerated fiche print-out illustrated on page 60 to see how much can be learnt about his family. This fiche provides the information as shown on the census return, including the precise address, with some abbreviations and contractions due to the constraints of the computer program.

Bibliography

Marriage, Census & Other Indexes, 6th edition, Jeremy Gibson & Elizabeth Hampson. FFHS, 1996.

Current Publications by Member Societies, 9th edition, ed. J.P.Perkins. FFHS, 1997.

Current Publications on Microfiche by Member Societies, 4th edition, ed. J.P. Perkins. FFHS, 1997.

IGI on Computer: the International Genealogical Index from CD ROM, David Hawgood (author and publisher), 1998.

Genealogy in the Computer Age: Understanding FamilySearch, Elizabeth Nichols. SLC, 1994. (Available from SoG.)

1881 CENSUS-SURNAME INDEX, COUNTY: SURREY

PELLING , Elizabeth PAGE: 19315

SURNAME	FORENAME	AGE	SEX	RELATIONSHIP TO HEAD	MARITAL CONDITION	CENSUS PLACE	OCCUPATION	NAME OF HEAD	WHERE BORN CO	WHERE BORN PARISH	NOTE	PUBLIC RECORD OFFICE PIECE RG11/	FOLIO NO	PAGE NO	G.S.U. FILM NUMBER
PELLING	Elizabeth	15	F	Serv	U	Reigate Borough	General Domes+	GRIGGS, Benjamin	SUR	Reigate		0799	87	8	1341188
PELLING	Ellen	28	F	Serv	U	Leatherhead	Cook Domestic+	TAYLOR, Peter	SUR	Ockley Parish		0763	9	11	1341179
PELLING	Ellen	19	F	Serv	U	Croydon	Gen Servant	RITCHIE, Walter W.	SUR	Reigate		0819	73	12	1341193
PELLING	Emily	20	F	Serv	U	Capel	Domestic Serv	HEATH, Douglas D.	SUS	Newtimber		0794	14	21	1341187
PELLING	Emma	30	F	Wife	M	Battersea	---	PELLING, John	MID	Islington		0655	115	3	1341152
PELLING	Emma	11	F	Daur	U	Lambeth	---	PELLING, George	SUR	Lambeth		0606	7	10	1341139
PELLING	Ernest	5m	M	Son	-	Battersea	---	PELLING, William	SUR	Battersea		0655	87	11	1341152
PELLING	Eva	12	F	Daur	U	Lambeth	---	PELLING, George	SUR	Lambeth		0606	7	10	1341139
PELLING	Fanny	33	F	Daur	U	Chobham	---	PELLING, John	SUR	Pirbright		0771	79	16	1341181
PELLING	Flora	8	F	Daur	-	Lambeth	---	PELLING, George	SUR	Lambeth		0606	8	11	1341139
PELLING	Florence	1m	F	GChd	-	Putney	---	PELLING, Mary	SUR	Putney		0661	54	3	1341153
PELLING	Frances	72	F	MotL	M	Clapham	---	SIMPKINS, Richard	KEN	Hoo		0634	127	6	1341146
PELLING	Frances J.	10	F	Niec	-	Newington	Scholar	LISLE, Joseph Wm.	MID	Finsbury		0538	118	16	1341127
PELLING	Francis	50	M	Head	M	Godalming	Gardener	Self	SUR	Clapham		0779	105	5	[illegible]
PELLING	George	70	M	Head	W	Putney	No Occ	Self	SUS	---		0?61	111	33	[illegible]
PELLING	George	58	M	Head	M	Lambeth	Beer Merchant	Self	KEN	Chiddingstone		0606	7	10	1341139
PELLING	George	28	M	Lodg	U	Ockley	Brickmaker	JENKINS, Mark	SUR	Ewhurst		0794	46	16	1341187
PELLING	George	21	M	Son	U	Lambeth	Carman	PELLING, George	MID	Fulham		0606	7	10	1341139
PELLING	George	18	M	Son	U	Dorking	Domestic Serv+	PELLING, William	SUR	Dorking		0796	32	27	1341187
PELLING	George	17	M	Son	U	Putney	Plumber	PELLING, Mary	SUR	Putney		0661	54	3	1341153
PELLING	George A.	12	M	Son	-	Battersea	Office Boy	PELLING, William	SUS	Steyning		0655	87	11	1341152
PELLING	Grace	8	F	Daur	-	Battersea	Scholar	PELLING, William	SUS	Steyning		0655	87	11	1341152
PELLING	Harry	6	M	Son	-	Lambeth	---	PELLING, George	SUR	Lambeth		0606	8	11	1341139
PELLING	Harry G.	25	M	Neph	U	Croydon	Solicitors Ge+	DOWNS, Louisa	SUS	Chichester		0812	83	32	1341192
PELLING	Henry	24	M	Son	U	Godalming	---	PELLING, Francis	SUR	Clapham		0779	105	5	1341183
PELLING	Horace J.	10	M	Son	-	Battersea	Scholar	PELLING, William	SUS	Steyning		0655	87	11	1341152
PELLING	Infant	1m	F	GDau	-	Wotton	---	PELLING, John	SUR	Wotton		0794	104	1	1341187
PELLING	James	49	M	Head	M	Reigate Foreign	Gardener	Self	SUR	Wooton		0797	85	36	1341188
PELLING	James	16	M	Son	U	Reigate Foreign	Carpenters La+	PELLING, James	SUR	Dorking		0797	85	36	1341188
PELLING	James	3	M	Son	-	Cranleigh	---	PELLING, Levi	SUS	Rudgwick		0792	94	20	1341186
PELLING	Jane	54	F	Wife	M	Dorking	---	PELLING, William	SUR	Dorking		0796	31	26	1341187
PELLING	Jane	12	F	Daur	U	Dorking	Scholar	PELLING, William	SUR	Dorking		0796	32	27	1341187
PELLING	Jessie	13	F	Serv	-	Godalming	Domestic Serv+	DODGE, Marten W.	SUR	Godalming		0779	63	8	1341183
PELLING	John	65	M	Head	M	Chobham	Grocer & Meal+	Self	SUR	Rudgwick		0771	79	16	1341181
PELLING	John	55	M	Head	W	Wotton	Coachman	Self	SUR	Wotton		0794	104	1	1341187
PELLING	John	27	M	Head	M	Battersea	Coach Builder	Self	SUR	Ockley		0655	115	3	1341152
PELLING	John	9	M	Son	U	Reigate Foreign	Scholar	PELLING, James	SUR	Reigate		0797	85	36	1341188
PELLING	John A.	20	M	Son	U	Lambeth	Carpenter	PELLING, George	MID	Fulham		0606	7	10	1341139
PELLING	Kate	7	F	Daur	-	Godalming	---	PELLING, Francis	---	---		0779	105	5	1341183
PELLING	Levi	29	M	Head	M	Cranleigh	Ag Lab	Self	SUS	Rudgwick		0792	94	20	1341186
PELLING	Levi	2	M	Son	-	Cranleigh	---	PELLING, Levi	SUR	Cranleigh		0792	94	20	1341186
PELLING	Louisa	30	F	Daur	U	Battersea	Housekeeper	PELLING, William	MID	Marylebone		0655	41	75	1341152
PELLING	Louisa	16	F	Serv	U	Clapham	Housemaid Dom+	KERSHAW, Maria	SUR	Brighton		0631	65	4	1341145
PELLING	Louisa	2	F	Daur	-	Lambeth	---	PELLING, George	SUR	Lambeth		0606	8	11	1341139
PELLING	Margaret	38	F	Serv	M	Penge	Servant (Dom)	GRACE, Robert P.	SUR	Rigate		0823	74	17	1341194
PELLING	Margaret	19	F	Serv	U	Croydon	Domestic Serv+	JONES, Charles H.	SUR	Reigate		0818	8	10	1341193
PELLING	Marian A.	22	F	Wife	M	Horley	Blacksmith Wi+	PELLING, Alfred	SUS	Itchingfield		0801	108	31	1341189
PELLING	Mary	59	F	Wife	M	Chobham	---	PELLING, John	SUR	Rudgwick		0771	79	16	1341181
PELLING	Mary	42	F	Head	W	Putney	---	Self	SUR	Brockham		0661	54	3	1341153
PELLING	Mary	29	F	Wife	M	Cranleigh	---	PELLING, Levi	SUS	Loxwood		0792	94	20	1341186
PELLING	Mary	10	F	Daur	-	Godalming	Scholar	PELLING, Francis	SUR	Clapham		0779	105	5	1341183

+ = SEE ORIGINAL CENSUS FOR FULL DATA
m = MONTHS w = WEEKS d = DAYS
> = GREATER THAN < = LESS THAN
M = MARRIED U = UNMARRIED W = WIDOW(ER) D = DIVORCED O = OTHER
* = SEE MISCELLANEOUS NOTES

Surname fiche from 1881 Census Index

CHAPTER EIGHT

Civil Registration

General Notes:

The starting dates for civil registration vary widely; 1837 in England and Wales; 1855 in Scotland; 1864 in Ireland. All registration services charge for searches made by their staff and for the issue of certificates. As prices and rates vary from country to country, and tend to increase with very little warning, they are not quoted in this book. You are advised to check with the relevant office and ascertain what costs will be involved before you order any certificates.

Also ask precisely what you will be able to see if you visit the office in question. In some countries the indexes alone may be consulted; in others the original registers may be viewed. Far more material is available on microfilm and microfiche than was the case a few years ago so copies are more widely dispersed and you should not need to travel to, say, London or Edinburgh to view civil registration indexes.

England and Wales

Since 1 July 1837 all births, marriages and deaths should have been registered by the State but in the period between 1837 and 1874 the responsibility for this lay with the registrars rather than with the local people concerned and consequently some events, particularly births, escaped the net.

Registration Districts and Search Facilities

The country was (and is) divided into Registration Districts under the control of a Superintendent Registrar, who was the only person permitted to solemnise civil marriages (today deputy SRs can also officiate). The original Registration Districts were based on the 1834 Poor Law Unions (see Chapter 11) and were then divided into sub-districts run by a Registrar. Copy certificates are available from the Registrar only at the time of registration or shortly afterwards; when a sub-district register is full it is sent to the Superintendent Registrar. Quarterly, Superintendent Registrars send copies of entries in their registers for the preceding three months to the Registrar General and from these returns the national indexes of births, marriages and deaths are compiled – usually known as GRO (General Register Office) Indexes.

Boundaries and names of Registration Districts may well have been altered several times since 1837 and this should be borne in mind when searching for an event. Some Registration Districts ceased to exist with local government re-organisation in 1974 and 1996 and their records were dispersed – for example, Wharfedale RD, in the West Riding of Yorkshire, disappeared and its records were split between the Registration Districts of Leeds and Bradford. You will often find staff helpful in passing on an incorrect request to another office.

If you are sure that your ancestors came from a particular area within a given Registration District then it may be easier, quicker and more convenient to search locally. You will find the address in the telephone directory under Registration of Births, Deaths & Marriages. First obtain an application form and fill it in as far as possible. If you do not know the exact date, you are entitled to ask the Registrar to search a 5-year period - a given date and two years either side of this. Register Offices do not have sufficient staff to undertake indefinite or protracted searches. If such a search is required then a general search in the indexes may be made personally, *provided that the office can accommodate you,* but it is relatively expensive and often not the most advantageous way of going about things as by the 19th century very few of our ancestors restricted their movements to one Registration District.

Before undertaking a general search locally, you should consider the advantages of a search of the National Indexes of Births Marriages and Deaths. Until comparatively recently, there was little choice but to travel to London to consult the indexes, or to find someone to do it for you. Now, however, microfilm or microfiche copies of all or part of the indexes are available at many libraries, record offices, some societies and all LDS Family History Centres. Check details of holdings in advance; many repositories have incomplete coverage of the 20th century indexes, most require that you book a film/fiche reader in advance, and some charge a search fee.

There have recently been considerable changes in the organisation and location of the central offices dealing with civil registration. The General Register Office is now part of the Office for National Statistics. A set of the National Indexes in book form (and on microfiche for disabled searchers : book in advance) is held at The Family Records Centre, 1 Myddelton Street, Islington, London EC1R 1UW, where they can be freely consulted.

The Family Records Centre also holds records relating to adoptions (from 1927), and Miscellaneous Indexes (also on microfiche elsewhere) which include many dealing with the armed services and from British Consulates and High Commissions. The earliest of these dates from 1761 but many only start in the late 19th or early 20th century.

Searching the Indexes and Ordering Copy Certificates

Separate indexes are kept for Births, Marriages and Deaths. There are four quarterly indexes for each year: ending 31 March, 30 June, 30 September and 31 December and covering events registered in the previous three months. It is important to note that the quarterly index in which the event appears is dependent on the date of registration and **not** on the date when the event took place. It may, therefore, be necessary to search the following quarter even when the precise date is known. The index gives the name, Registration District (but **not** place where the event occurred), volume and page number. Note that these reference numbers relate to the GRO records only and are of no use when applying to a local Register Office for a certificate. There may be two or more entries for the same name in different Districts and you may not know in which county the place of registration is located. This can be ascertained from the list on page 39. For example, XX for the year 1849 indicates that the event took place in Lancashire; 8a for the year 1860 places the event in Cheshire. If you are uncertain whether the reference you have found in the index relates to the person you are seeking then it can be checked for you within a few days by reference to the records on payment of a sum which is about half the cost of a certificate. Once you have found the entry which you believe is the one you want, a simple form must be completed. Certificates ordered in person from the Family Records Centre can normally be collected on the fourth subsequent working day or can be posted to you. A priority service is available here upon payment of a fee almost four times the normal cost of a certificate whereby it can be collected the day after application. The cost of a certificate is the same locally or nationally. If you cannot visit the Family Records Centre to make a personal search, certificates may be applied for by post. If you can supply the exact GRO index reference (Quarter; Year; District; Volume number; Page number) the cost is half as much again as a certificate ordered in person; otherwise a five year search can be requested and an additional sum has to be paid. It may therefore be cheaper to pay someone to carry out the personal search for you, if their fee is less than the difference.

Postal applications should be sent to: General Register Office, PO Box 2, Southport, Merseyside PR8 2JD. Cheques and postal orders should be made payable to the Office for National Statistics. Payment by credit/debit card is acceptable; cash should **not** be sent. Remittances from overseas should be by sterling money order. You should allow 28 days for delivery of certificates.

Points to bear in mind:

General

Certificates will only be issued if the details given on them match **exactly** those on your application form. Consider the possible problems on page 52 before filling in the details. Remember that occupations were flexible – a labourer might be put down as such on one certificate but may be a farm servant or a woodman on others; a miner could describe himself as a collier, a hewer or even an excavator.

Births: are reported to the Registrar by individuals, usually close relatives.

When ordering a birth certificate, a full one should always be requested – a short certificate does not contain all the information shown on page 50. The mother's maiden name is shown in the indexes **after** September 1911. Parents were allowed 42 days to register a birth free of charge, after which a fee was payable. Thus a birth on December 26 may not have been registered until the March quarter of the following year and the birth date may have been 'adjusted' to bring it within the limit.

A direct ancestor's birth certificate may not always be the best one to obtain. To explain this statement it is necessary to anticipate slightly the contents of the next Chapter. Census returns may be consulted (free of charge) for the years 1841, 1851, 1861, 1871, 1881 and 1891, but it is necessary to know an address. Suppose that your grandfather, Malcolm, had been born in 1866, his sister Nichola in 1863 and his brother David in 1870. The essential information you require (names of parents and mother's maiden name) should be the same on the birth certificates for all three, but by obtaining David's (instead of Malcolm's) you will have an address to check in the 1871 census. The family is less likely to have moved in the intervening year after 1870 than in the 5 years after 1866.

Marriages: it is normally easier to find a marriage, and to be almost certain that you are right, than to find a birth because each partner is indexed under their own name. Look for the less common name first then check it with the name of the spouse and, if the references are identical, you will usually have a match. **After** 1912 each partner's surname is included in the entry for the other one. Bear in mind that if the bride is a widow, the name in the index will be her married surname, not her maiden surname.

Church of England: since 1837 two identical copies of Anglican marriage registers have been kept by ministers. When the books are full, one is retained by the Church and the other deposited at the Register Office. The register for a small parish in which there are few marriages per year may take a very long time to complete (some begun in 1837 are still in use) and the Superintendent may, therefore, not have a copy of the register. The present record-keeping methods in most local offices, particularly urban ones, make it difficult to trace a marriage unless the church is known.

Jews and Quakers: did not need a Registrar present after 1837 but had to conform to the statutory regulations.

Other Religious Denominations: from 1837 could apply for their churches or chapels to be registered for marriages but until 1899 a registrar had to be present and the marriage was recorded in the register belonging to the local register office. From 1899, nonconformist congregations could keep their own marriage registers.

Civil Marriages: are registered when they are performed and entered in the local register office's register. This applies to marriages in licensed places (such as hotels or stately homes) as well as to those taking place in the register office itself.

Deaths: English death certificates are not as helpful genealogically as Scottish or Australasian ones but they are worth obtaining. They can provide an address for checking in the census returns, give an approximate age at death from which one can compute a birth date (from 1866 onwards the indexes include age at death) and sometimes confirm a relationship. When ordering a pre-1866 death certificate it may be advisable to provide a possible age range – the informant was often a close relative but many people even today are hard put to it to give an accurate age for an elderly relative and before 1866 few people would have written proof of their age. Watch for a daughter whose married surname was unknown to you or the remarriage of a mother when a son from her first marriage is the informant.

No.	When and where born	Names if any	Sex	Name and surname of father	Name, surname and maiden surname of mother	Occupation of father	Signature, description and residence of informant	When registered	Signature of Registrar	Name entered after Registration

Data given in birth certificates

No.	When married	Names & surnames of each party	Ages	Condition (e.g. Bachelor or Spinster)	Rank or Profession	Residence at time of marriage	Both Fathers' names & surnames	Rank or profession of both Fathers
Place of marriage, by whom ceremony was performed and whether after banns, licence or certificate								
Signatures of parties who were married					Signatures of witnesses			

Data given in marriage cerificates

No.	When & where died	Name & surname	Sex	Age (often only approximate)	Occupation	Cause	Signature description & residence of informant	When registered	Signature of Registrar

Data given in death certificates

The birth and marriage certificates shown on page 51 illustrate the point made about names on page 52. The birth of **ALEXANDER PELLING** was registered by his mother, Ann, who, it will be seen, made her mark.

The Registrar recorded her maiden name as **BIRFETT**. The marriage indexes were searched backwards from 1855 for 10 years and forward for 5 (marriages do not always precede births). No marriage between **MICHAEL PELLING** and **ANN BIRFETT** was registered. Fortunately, there was only one **MICHAEL PELLING** who married in the period. The certificate illustrated was obtained and his wife's name proved to be **BURFOOT**; in the index it is listed as **BURFOTT**!

The searcher did not know at the time that his aunt, who never knew her grandparents, had a sampler completed by **ANN BURFOOT** in 1826. This demonstrates the importance of family information, which has already been stressed. It also shows that girls who embroidered samplers including their names were not necessarily literate but may simply have copied or filled in a pattern provided.

The death certificate was important because it provided an address to look for in the 1861 census (see Chapter 9) without which Michael's birthplace would have been more difficult to find.

Civil Registration

CERTIFIED COPY OF AN ENTRY OF BIRTH

The fee for this certificate is 40p. When application is made by post a handling fee is payable in addition.

GIVEN AT THE GENERAL REGISTER OFFICE, SOMERSET HOUSE, LONDON

Application Number 3716

REGISTRATION DISTRICT Hambledon

1855. BIRTH in the Sub-district of Cranley in the County of Surrey

Columns:— No.	1 When and where born	2 Name, if any	3 Sex	4 Name and surname of father	5 Name, surname and maiden surname of mother	6 Occupation of father	7 Signature, description and residence of informant	8 When registered	9 Signature of registrar	10* Name entered after registration
291	Tenth July 1855 Pitland Street Ewhurst	Alexander	Boy	Michael Pelling	Ann Pelling formerly Burfett	Agricultural Labourer	X The Mark of Ann Pelling Mother Pitland Street Ewhurst	Twentieth August 1855	James [illegible] Registrar	—

CERTIFIED to be a true copy of an entry in the certified copy of a Register of Births in the District above mentioned.
Given at the GENERAL REGISTER OFFICE, SOMERSET HOUSE, LONDON, under the Seal of the said Office, the 30th day of June 1972

*See note overleaf

This certificate is issued in pursuance of the Births and Deaths Registration Act 1953. Section 34 provides that any certified copy of an entry purporting to be sealed or stamped with the seal of the General Register Office shall be received as evidence of the birth or death to which it relates without any further or other proof of the entry, and no certified copy purporting to have been given in the said Office shall be of any force or effect unless it is sealed or stamped as aforesaid.

BX 886648

CAUTION:—Any person who (1) falsifies any of the particulars on this certificate, or (2) uses a falsified certificate as true, knowing it to be false, is liable to prosecution.

Form A502M (S.331201) Dd. 633398 90,000 12/71 Hw. RE-30

CERTIFIED COPY OF AN ENTRY OF MARRIAGE

The fee for this certificate is 40p. When application is made by post, a handling fee is payable in addition.

Given at the GENERAL REGISTER OFFICE, SOMERSET HOUSE, LONDON

Application Number 4675D

Registration District Horsham

1846. Marriage solemnized at the Church in the Parish of Horsham in the County of Sussex

No.	1 When married	2 Name and surname	3 Age	4 Condition	5 Rank or profession	6 Residence at the time of marriage	7 Father's name and surname	8 Rank or profession of father
251	March 17	Michael Pelling	full	Bachelor	Labourer	Horsham	John Pelling	Farmer
		Ann Burfoot	full	Spinster	—	Horsham	Alexander Burfoot	Farmer

Married in the Parish Church according to the Rites and Ceremonies of the Church of England by Banns by me

This marriage was solemnized between us, Michael Pelling, Ann Burfoot

in the presence of us, R. Collins, Elizabeth Burfoot

John F. Hodgson Vicar

Form A513 (S.330809) Dd.833394 30,000 10/71 Hw.

CERTIFIED to be a true copy of an entry in the certified copy of a Register of Marriages in the District above mentioned.
Given at the GENERAL REGISTER OFFICE, SOMERSET HOUSE, LONDON, under the Seal of the said Office, the 13th day of July 1972.

This certificate is issued in pursuance of section 65 of the Marriage Act 1949. Sub-section (3) of that section provides that any certified copy of an entry purporting to be sealed or stamped with the seal of the General Register Office shall be received as evidence of the marriage to which it relates without any further or other proof of the entry, and no certified copy purporting to have been given in the said Office shall be of any force or effect unless it is sealed or stamped as aforesaid.

MA 983416

CAUTION:—Any person who (1) falsifies any of the particulars on this certificate, or (2) uses a falsified certificate as true knowing it to be false, is liable to prosecution.

CERTIFIED COPY OF AN ENTRY OF DEATH

GIVEN AT THE GENERAL REGISTER OFFICE, SOMERSET HOUSE, LONDON

Application Number 5158.D

REGISTRATION DISTRICT Hambledon

1861. DEATH in the Sub-district of Cranley in the County of Surrey

Columns:— No.	1 When and where died	2 Name and surname	3 Sex	4 Age	5 Occupation	6 Cause of death	7 Signature, description and residence of informant	8 When registered	9 Signature of registrar
190	Seventeenth April 1861 Pitland Street Ewhurst	Michael Pelling	Male	43 Years	Farm Labourer	Pneumonia of the right Lung certified	Ebenezer Howden In Attendance Cranley Street Cranley	Eighteenth April 1861	Edward Davey Registrar

CERTIFIED to be a true copy of an entry in the certified copy of a Register of Deaths in the District above mentioned.
Given at the GENERAL REGISTER OFFICE, SOMERSET HOUSE, LONDON, under the Seal of the said Office, the 13th day of Sept 19.73

This certificate is issued in pursuance of the Births and Deaths Registration Act 1953. Section 34 provides that any certified copy of an entry purporting to be sealed or stamped with the seal of the General Register Office shall be received as evidence of the birth or death to which it relates without any further or other proof of the entry, and no certified copy purporting to have been given in the said Office shall be of any force or effect unless it is sealed or stamped as aforesaid.

DX 190002

CAUTION:—Any person who (1) falsifies any of the particulars on this certificate, or (2) uses a falsified certificate as true, knowing it to be false, is liable to prosecution.

13/9/73

Facsimiles of certificates as issued by the General Register Office

Problems:

If you do not find the entry that you expect at a particular date there are many possible reasons. Among the most common are:

(a) **The date you have is wrong** – a frequent occurrence.
Remedy: widen your search progressively either side of the date you expected to find the entry. Search all four quarters of the year in question and then, say, five years before and five years after.

(b) **The name is different.**
Remedies:
  (i) look for all possible spelling variants of the surname. Remember that your ancestor may have been illiterate and the verbal information he gave may have been misheard or misspelt. This happens with common surnames as well as with the more unusual. A researcher in Lancashire has recorded no fewer than 17 different spellings of Whittaker. The difference may be much greater than a missing or extra letter. The name of one of my grandparents was Passiful, which in many records appears as Percival. Be especially careful of names beginning with 'H' or a vowel – many an Ardern has been recorded as Hardern and Hiles as Iles.
  (ii) consider illegitimacy – is a child registered at birth under the mother's maiden surname?
  (iii) look under all possible combinations of Christian names. Your grandfather may have been registered as Nehemiah John but always been known as Jack; your uncle Eric may have been registered as Fred*eric*k; cousin Joe may have been registered as just that and not as the expected Joseph.

(c) **The event was not registered.**
Remedy: make sure you have not fallen into any of the traps suggested above. If the missing entry is for a girl before 1874 look for a possible registration for a brother – there is some evidence that parents in the early years were more particular about registering boys. Consider whether the event could have taken place elsewhere, say in Scotland, or overseas (particularly if the man was in one of the armed services).

Scotland

Registration did not become compulsory in Scotland until 1855, but Scottish certificates have always been more detailed than English and Welsh ones.

In addition to the information given on English certificates, the following is usually stated:

  (i) **Birth.** Date and place of parents' marriage (in 1855 and from 1861 onwards). (1855 certificates only also state parents' ages and birthplaces.)
  (ii) **Marriage.** For both parties; name of mother + her maiden surname.
  (iii) **Death.** Both parents' names + mother's maiden name.

The Registers of Births, Marriages and Deaths are at New Register House in Edinburgh. Here the original entries may be consulted on microfiche, not just the indexes as in England. NRH also holds the census returns for Scotland and most of the surviving Old Parish Registers 1553-1854 (consultation of both is from microform). The indexes of BMD and the OPR indexes are available on computer and, having located the desired index reference, the microfilm/microfiche can be self-accessed. A very helpful factor is that the Scottish registration service has a system of district reference numbering with a format similar to that shown on page 39 for England and Wales and the same referencing system and numbers are used for the OPRs and for census returns. See page 29 for Internet information.

A fee is payable to work in New Register House (with daily/weekly/monthly/quarterly/annual rates) and as accommodation in the search rooms is limited you are strongly recommended to book prior to a visit. Enquiries as to the cost of copy certificates by personal application or by post should be made to NRH.

Microfilm copies of the **indexes** (1855-1920) are held at the Society of Genealogists and at Family History Centres. Access to all the indexes is also available by a computer inter-link system at the Family Records Centre at Myddelton Place: booking necessary and a fee payable to use this facility. Certificates must be ordered from NRH.

Other records available for consultation on microfilm and microfiche include the adopted children register (from 1930), register of divorces (from 1984) and a similar series of Miscellaneous Indexes to those in England, dealing with the services and records from British Consulates and High Commissions.

Ireland

Complete registration did not begin in Ireland until 1 January 1864 although non-Catholic marriages were registered from 1 April 1845. Registers of births, marriages and deaths before 31 December 1921 for the whole of Ireland, and after that date for the Republic of Ireland only, are held at the General Register Office in Dublin. Records for Northern Ireland, from 1 January 1922, are separate (see below).

The indexes are available for public search on payment of a fee – unlike England, Wales and Scotland where searching these is free of charge. The original registers have been microfilmed and printouts from these may be obtained for considerably less than the cost of a full certificate but they are for information only and have no legal standing. Births 1864-1867 are included in the IGI (see Chapter 7). The office also holds a similar series of Miscellaneous Indexes to those held in England and Scotland, with the Adopted Children Register beginning in 1953.

Northern Ireland

(Counties of Antrim, Armagh, Down, Fermanagh, Londonderry and Tyrone)

Registrations of births, marriages and deaths since 1922 are held at the General Register Office for Northern Ireland in Belfast. The indexes are open for public research by appointment only (well in advance). A similar series of Miscellaneous Indexes, mostly dating from 1922, is here.

Original marriage registers for Northern Ireland to 1921 are held by local registrars.

(N.B. Overseas researchers should note that neither General Register Office holds emigration records.)

Channel Islands

Jersey

Registration began in August 1842. No personal searches may be made. Access to the indexes is through the Superintendent Registrar in St Helier.

Guernsey and the other Islands

Personal searches may be made at the office of the Registrar General in St Peter Port, who holds all the civil registration records, with indexes, for these islands. The registers themselves may be consulted; not just the indexes.

Registration of births and deaths for Guernsey, Herm and Jethou commenced in October 1840 with non-Anglican marriages being added in January 1841. Marriages solemnised in the Anglican Church were not registered with the civil authorities until 1919. Before 1925 civil registers for Alderney and Sark were maintained by local registrars on the islands; after 1925 by the Registrar General on Guernsey.

Isle of Man

Although registration of births was not compulsory until 1878, an Act of 1849 provided that 'persons who object to and decline the offices of the Established Church' could register births and marriages. The earliest contemporary records therefore date from 1849 but it was also provided that earlier births could be registered, on oath, and the earliest of the 46 recorded under this provision was 1821. Marriages were not centrally registered until 1884. The Civil Registry holds civil registers for the whole island. Microfilm copies of the registers are in the Manx Museum Library.

Bibliography

Introduction to Civil Registration, Tom Wood. FFHS, 1994.

District Register Offices in England & Wales, 13th edition. E.Yorkshire FHS, 1997.

People Count: a history of the General Register Office, Muriel Nissel. London HMSO, 1987.

The Parishes, Registers & Registrars of Scotland. Scottish Association of Family History Societies, 1993.

See also Bibliography to Chapter 5.

CHAPER NINE

Census Returns

A census – an official, detailed account of all inhabitants – has been taken in each area of the British Isles every 10 years since 1801 (except 1941). Apart from some local variations the format used is the same in all areas – for example, the 1881 census for Scotland identifies Gaelic speakers, the 1891 for Wales and Monmouthshire asks whether people speak English, Welsh or both languages – but examples used here are taken from England. It was not until 1841 that the returns had to be preserved. Consequently, for the previous four censuses, only the official statistics remain. Occasionally, however, the earlier returns did survive and whilst it is true to say that, generally speaking, the first census of practical use to the family historian is 1841, you should check to see if you are one of those fortunate researchers whose ancestors lived in an area for which earlier returns have been found; see the Bibliography for books listing these.

The following example of a rare survival of an 1801 census for Winwick with Hulme (one of the ten townships of the Parish of Winwick, originally in Lancashire, now in Cheshire), includes a farmer aged 74, who was therefore born about 1727.

Ralph	**Unsworth** Sen.	74	Farmer
Nancey	**Unsworth**	38	
Ralph	**Unsworth**	11	
Peter	**Unsworth**	9	
John	**Unsworth**	7	
Robt	**Unsworth**	4	
Marshall	**Brown**	19	Servant
Margret	**Gorst**	18	Servant

Certain records, including censuses, which contain sensitive personal information, are subject to extended closure and do not become available for 100 years. The latest census which can currently be consulted in person is therefore 1891 – apart from Ireland, see page 61.

The Registrar General's Office will extract the ages and places of birth of named persons at a specific address in the 1901 census for England and Wales, provided that written permission of the person(s), or a direct descendant, is produced and a declaration must be signed that the information will not be used in litigation. Applications, on a special form, should be made to the Office for National Statistics, Room 4324, Segensworth Road, Titchfield, Hampshire PO15 5RR. This procedure is expensive and therefore advisable only if there is no alternative source.

continued on page 58

PLACE	HOUSES: Uninhabited or Building	HOUSES: Inhabited	NAMES of each Person who abode therein the preceding Night.	AGE and SEX: Males	AGE and SEX: Females	PROFESSION, TRADE, EMPLOYMENT, or of INDEPENDENT MEANS.	Where Born: Whether Born in same County	Where Born: Whether Born in Scotland, Ireland, or Foreign Parts.
Vicarage		1	Geo. Matthews	40		Vicar	Y	
			Willm do	35		Ind	"	
			Rebecca do		45	do	"	
			Sarah do		45		"	
			Catherine do		20		"	
			Jas. Redaway	40		Engraver	"	
			Martha do		15	Ind	"	
			Hester Buck		14	F S	Y	
Alabaster		1	Danl. Burger	55		Ag lab	"	
			Elizabeth do		50		"	
			Miriam Tanage		11	F S	"	
Common		1	George Port	30		Bricklayer	"	
			Mary do		25		"	
			Peter do	4			"	
			Mary do		2		"	
			Mary Sayers		13	F S	"	
do		1	Noah Pelling	30		Ag lab	"	
			Ann do		25		"	
			Willm do	6			"	
			Henry do	5			"	
			John do	3			"	
			Harriett do		1		"	
			Phillis do		9		"	
			Thos. Andrew	60		Ag lab	"	
Freeth.r		1	Thos. Parker	53		—	"	
TOTAL in Page 13		5		12	13			

Extract from the 1841 census (HO 107/1092) Rudgwick, Sussex

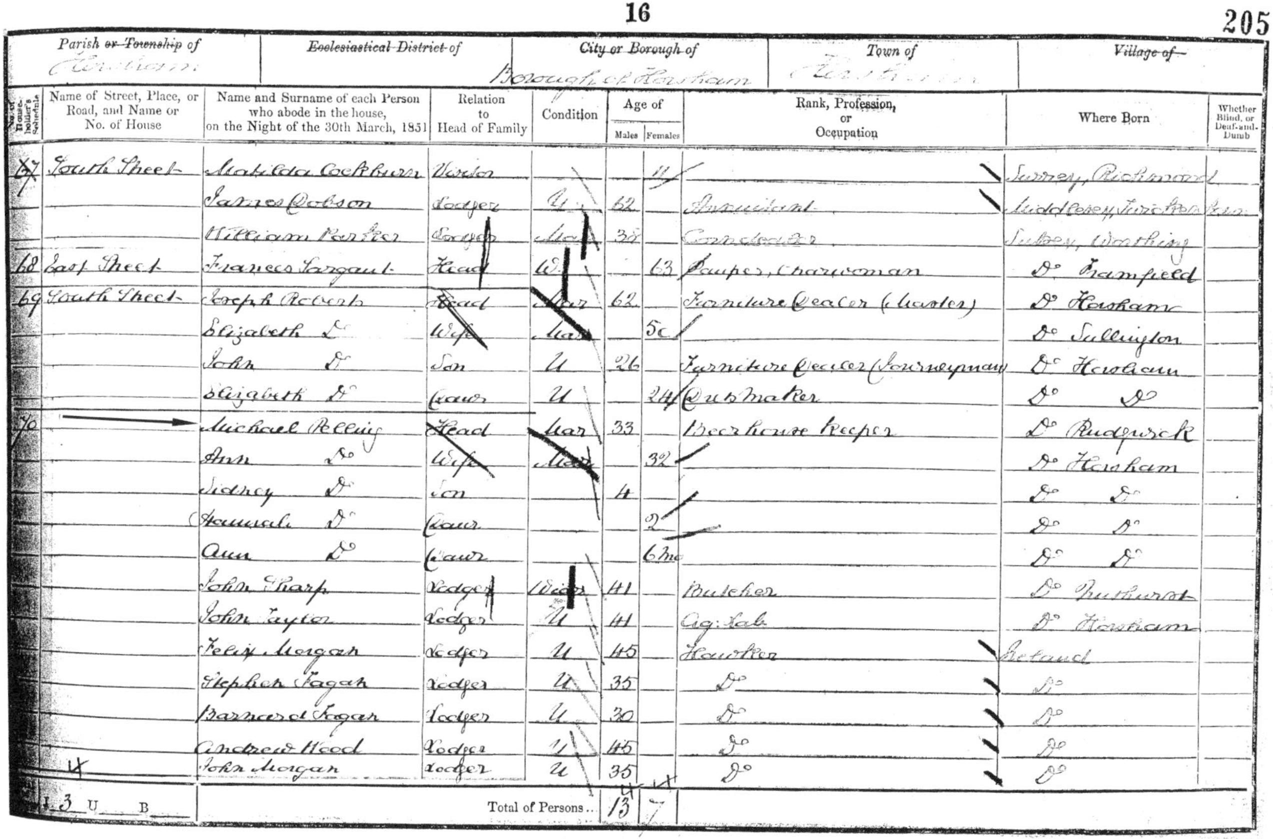

16 205

Parish ~~or Township~~ of Horsham	~~Ecclesiastical District~~ of	City ~~or Borough~~ of Borough of Horsham	Town of Horsham	~~Village of~~					
No. of House-holder's Schedule	Name of Street, Place, or Road, and Name or No. of House	Name and Surname of each Person who abode in the house, on the Night of the 30th March, 1851	Relation to Head of Family	Condition	Age of Males	Age of Females	Rank, Profession, or Occupation	Where Born	Whether Blind, or Deaf-and-Dumb
67	South Street	Matilda Cockburn	Visitor			11		Surrey, Richmond	
		James Dobson	Lodger	U	62		Annuitant	Middlesex, [illegible]	
		William Parker	Lodger	Mar	38		Coachbuilder	Sussex, Worthing	
68	East Street	Frances Sargant	Head	W		63	Pauper, Charwoman	Do Frampfield	
69	South Street	Joseph Roberts	Head	Mar	62		Furniture Dealer (Master)	Do Horsham	
		Elizabeth Do	Wife	Mar		50		Do Sullington	
		John Do	Son	U	26		Furniture Dealer (Journeyman)	Do Horsham	
		Elizabeth Do	Daur	U		24	Dressmaker	Do Do	
70		Michael Relling	Head	Mar	33		Beerhouse Keeper	Do Rudgwick	
		Ann Do	Wife	Mar		32		Do Horsham	
		Sidney Do	Son		4			Do Do	
		Hannah Do	Daur			2		Do Do	
		Ann Do	Daur			6 mo		Do Do	
		John Sharp	Lodger	Widr	41		Butcher	Do Rusthurst	
		John Taylor	Lodger	U	41		Ag: Lab	Do Horsham	
		Felix Morgan	Lodger	U	45		Hawker	Ireland	
		Stephen Fagan	Lodger	U	35		Do	Do	
		Barnard Fagan	Lodger	U	30		Do	Do	
		Andrew Wood	Lodger	U	45		Do	Do	
		John Morgan	Lodger	U	35		Do	Do	
3 U B				Total of Persons	13	7			

Extract from the 1851 census (HO 107/1648) Horsham, Sussex

Census Returns

Of the census returns which you will be using, it is easier to describe the later ones first. The returns for 1851, taken on the night of 30 March, 1861 on 7 April, 1871 2 April, 1881 3 April, 1891 5 April (one day later in Scotland between 1841 and 1881) all give the following information:

(a) Name of Place, Parish, and whether hamlet, village, town or borough.
(b) Number or name of house and its street or road; some enumerators, particularly in rural areas, simply entered the schedule number and not the house number – the two should not be confused.
(c) Names of persons present on Census night (dates as above).
(d) Relationship of each person to the Head of the Household.
(e) Matrimonial status.
(f) Age and sex.
(g) Rank, profession or occupation.
(h) Birthplace: England and Wales by place and county, but generally country only (e.g. Scotland) for those born elsewhere. The same applies in reverse – a Scottish census will often just give 'England'. 'N.K.' means Not Known. 'N.B.' is sometimes used for North Britain (i.e. Scotland).
(j) Whether blind, deaf or dumb (1871 included whether imbecile, idiot or lunatic).

The 1841 (6 June) census was unfortunately not so informative in several respects; using the letters above:
(b) Very few streets were numbered.
(d) Relationship to the Head of the Household not stated.
(e) Not given.
(f) Ages for those above 15 rounded down to nearest 5 years below (e.g. recorded age 45; actual age could be 45, 46, 47, 48 or 49). Ages for those over 60 can be unreliable; they were sometimes rounded down to the nearest 10 years and the exact ages of many were unknown so were estimated.
(h) Birthplace indicated by an initial 'Y[es]' if born in the same county in which the person was then living, 'N[o]' if elsewhere in England and Wales. Those born in Scotland, Ireland or Foreign Parts listed as such by initials; people living elsewhere in the British Isles but born in England shown as 'E'.

The differences between 1841 and 1851 (and later censuses) can be seen from the examples on pages 56 and 57.

The marks made by enumerators should be noted:

/ at the end of each household.

// at the end of each building.

The exception is the 1851 census in which a line was drawn across the first 4 columns after the end of the building and a shorter line after the household.

Microfilmed (and, for 1891 only, microfiched) copies of the censuses for England, Wales, the Channel Islands and the Isle of Man are available for inspection on the first floor of the Family Records Centre (for details and opening times see page 27). It is recommended that you read ***Making Use of the Census*** (see Bibliography). For other areas see below.

Complete holdings of the various censuses for a county will usually be found in the County Record Office or the main county library and many reference libraries have copies for their local area, on microfilm or microfiche.

It is preferable to know an address to research a town with reasonable hope of quick success, although if the district in the town is known and this coincides with the sub-districts, you will find these listed on the title page of each enumerator's book and the amount of searching can be confined. At the Family Records Centre in London there are street indexes covering 1841-1891 for all London Registration Districts, all towns with a population in the nineteenth century of 40,000 or more, and some smaller areas. Preston, in Lancashire, is street indexed from 1851; within Preston Registration District, Enumeration Districts vary in size considerably with the largest having 325 houses with 2,164 inhabitants, the smallest 114 with 616. Many record offices, libraries and Family History Centres hold copies of street indexes for their own areas – always ask if one is available as they are not always kept on open shelves. In rural areas it is generally possible to research whole villages and the surrounding countryside relatively quickly.

Many Societies have indexed the 1851 census for their area, some by surname only, others including much more information, and most publish the results in booklet or microfiche format; approximately 90% of England and Wales is currently covered in some form. In some areas the other censuses have been, or are being, indexed. You should request a publications leaflet from the appropriate society or see ***Current Publications,*** details on page 44.

The biggest and most ambitious project of all, however, begun in 1988 and completed in 1996, was to index the whole of the 1881 census for England and Wales. Scotland was included later. For more details of this see Chapter 7.

When using census returns

If you cannot find the address bear in mind that the street, name or house numbers may have been changed between the date of the record you have and the date of the census. A local directory (see Chapter 14) may help to solve the problem.

All details on censuses should be noted including visitors and servants. When girls married and left home, or families moved to a new area, they often continued to obtain servants from their original home area and a servant's birthplace can, therefore, sometimes provide a clue to a family's place of origin. Boarders or lodgers may also prove to be family members.

The experienced family historian will not confine himself to one surname but will make a comprehensive search looking for the surnames of married daughters and wives' maiden names. He will also note down the neighbours, not only to provide

1881 CENSUS-AS ENUMERATED, COUNTY: SURREY

Ockley , 0794 45 14 PAGE: 22671

CENSUS DATA © BRITISH CROWN COPYRIGHT 1982.
MICROFICHE EDITION OF THE INDEXES © COPYRIGHT 1990, BY CORPORATION OF THE PRESIDENT OF THE CHURCH OF JESUS CHRIST OF LATTER-DAY SAINTS.

CENSUS PLACE	HOUSEHOLD		SURNAME	RELATIONSHIP TO HEAD		MARITAL CONDITION				WHERE BORN		NOTE	REFERENCES			
	ADDRESS			FORENAME			AGE	SEX	OCCUPATION	CO	PARISH		PUBLIC RECORD OFFICE PIECE ROLL/	FOLIO NO	PAGE NO	G.S.U. FILM NUMBER
Ockley	Wolverstone Co+		DUNN	John Prince	Lodg	U	23	M	Gardener (D)	OXF	Adderbury		0794	45	14	1341187
Ockley	Woodgers Cotta+	//	SCHOLEY	George	Head	M	50	M	Gamekeeper	LIN	Scopwick		0794	45	14	1341187
Ockley	Woodgers Cotta+		SCHOLEY	Ann	Wife	M	41	F	Wife	LIN	Swarby		0794	45	14	1341187
Ockley	Woodgers Cotta+		SCHOLEY	George	Son	U	18	M	Under Gamekee+	YKS	Sandale		0794	45	14	1341187
Ockley	Woodgers Cotta+		SCHOLEY	Sarah Ann	Daur	U	14	F	Scholar	YKS	Loversall		0794	45	14	1341187
Ockley	Buckin Hill Fa+	//	AYLWOOD	John	Head	M	35	M	Agri Labr	SUR	Ockley		0794	45	14	1341187
Ockley	Buckin Hill Fa+		AYLWOOD	Grace	Wife	M	47	F	Wife	CON	---		0794	45	14	1341187
Ockley	Buckin Hill Fa+	//	WORSFOLD	Wm.	Head	M	48	M	Working Balif+	SUR	Cranleigh		0794	45	14	1341187
Ockley	Buckin Hill Fa+		WORSFOLD	Catherine	Wife	M	35	F	Wife	SUR	Ewhurst		0794	45	14	1341187
Ockley	Buckin Hill Fa+		WORSFOLD	Arthur	Son	U	13	M	Scholar	SUR	Lingfield		0794	45	14	1341187
Ockley	Buckin Hill Fa+		WORSFOLD	Catherine	Daur	U	11	F	Scholar	SUR	Lingfield		0794	45	14	1341187
Ockley	Buckin Hill Fa+		WORSFOLD	Sarah	Daur	U	10	F	Scholar	SUR	Lingfield		0794	45	14	1341187
Ockley	Buckin Hill Fa+		WORSFOLD	Walter	Son	U	8	M	Scholar	SUR	Lingfield		0794	46	15	1341187
Ockley	Buckin Hill Fa+		WORSFOLD	Fredk.	Son	U	1	M	---	SUR	Ockley		0794	46	15	1341187
Ockley	Buckin Hill Fa+	//	TAYLOR	John	Head	M	36	M	Shepherd	SUR	Westcot		0794	46	15	1341187
Ockley	Buckin Hill Fa+		TAYLOR	Hellen	Wife	M	30	F	Wife	BEK	Binfield		0794	46	15	1341187
Ockley	Buckin Hill Fa+		TAYLOR	John	Son	U	10	M	Scholar	SUR	Great Bookham		0794	46	15	1341187
Ockley	Buckin Hill Fa+		TAYLOR	Charles	Son	U	8	M	Scholar	BEK	Binfield		0794	46	15	1341187
Ockley	Buckin Hill Fa+		TAYLOR	Arthur	Son	U	4	M	Scholar	BEK	Grayley		0794	46	15	1341187
Ockley	Buckin Hill Fa+		TAYLOR	Elizabeth	Daur	U	2	F	---	SUR	Ockley		0794	46	15	1341187
Ockley	Buckin Hill Co+	//	BLUNDEN	John	Head	M	30	M	Carter	HAM	Petersfield		0794	46	15	1341187
Ockley	Buckin Hill Co+		BLUNDEN	Eliza	Wife	M	32	F	Wife	SUR	Lambeth		0794	46	15	1341187
Ockley	Buckin Hill Co+		BLUNDEN	Alice	Daur	U	9	F	Scholar	HAM	Petersfield		0794	46	15	1341187
Ockley	Buckin Hill Co+		BLUNDEN	John	Son	U	7	M	Scholar	HAM	Petersfield		0794	46	15	1341187
Ockley	Buckin Hill Co+		BLUNDEN	Alfred	Son	U	5	M	Scholar	SUS	West Grinstead		0794	46	15	1341187
Ockley	Buckin Hill Co+		BLUNDEN	Rosa	Daur	U	2	F	---	SUS	Henfield		0794	46	15	1341187
Ockley	Park Lodge	//	GADD	George	Head	M	46	M	Agri Labr	SUR	Newdigate		0794	46	15	1341187
Ockley	Park Lodge		GADD	Miriam	Wife	M	49	F	Wife	SUR	West Horsley		0794	46	15	1341187
Ockley	Park Lodge		GADD	George	Son	U	17	M	Agri Labr	SUR	Ockley		0794	46	15	1341187
Ockley	Park Lodge		GADD	Jesse	Son	U	9	M	Scholar	SUR	Ockley		0794	46	15	1341187
Ockley	Park Farm	//	DOARY	George	Head	M	41	M	Agri Lab	HAM	sobfern		0794	46	15	1341187
Ockley	Park Farm		DOARY	Rebbee	Wife	M	36	F	Wife	HAM	South Stoneham		0794	46	15	1341187
Ockley	Park Farm		DOARY	George	Son	U	9	M	Scholar	HAM	Fareham		0794	46	15	1341187
Ockley	Park Farm		DOARY	Elizabeth	Daur	U	7	F	Scholar	HAM	South Stoneham		0794	46	15	1341187
Ockley	Park Farm		DOARY	Sarah	Daur	U	4	F	Scholar	HAM	South Stoneham		0794	46	15	1341187
Ockley	Park Farm		DOARY	Peter	Son	U	2	M	---	SUR	Ockley		0794	46	15	1341187
Ockley	Park Farm	//	SAYERS	Wm.	Head	M	66	M	Agri Labr	SUR	Ockley		0794	46	16	1341187
Ockley	Park Farm		SAYERS	Caroline	Wife	M	60	F	Wife	SUR	Ockley		0794	46	16	1341187
Ockley	Park Farm		LONGHURST	Thomas	Lodg	M	54	M	Agri Labr	SUR	Ockley		0794	46	16	1341187
Ockley	Park Cottage	//	WHENHAM	Edward	Head	M	59	M	Occupier Bric+	KEN	Chatham		0794	46	16	1341187
Ockley	Park Cottage		WHENHAM	Ann	Wife	M	62	F	Wife	SUS	Horsham		0794	46	16	1341187
Ockley	Park Cottage		PELLING	Richard	SonL	U	24	M	Tile Maker	SUR	Ewhurst		0794	46	16	1341187
Ockley	Park Cottage	//	JENKINS	Mark	Head	M	32	M	Agri Labr	SUS	Slinfold		0794	46	16	1341187
Ockley	Park Cottage		JENKINS	Hannah	Wife	M	32	F	Wife	SUS	Horsham		0794	46	16	1341187
Ockley	Park Cottage		JENKINS	George	Son	U	11	M	Scholar	SUR	Abinger		0794	46	16	1341187
Ockley	Park Cottage		JENKINS	Anne	Daur	U	4	F	Scholar	SUR	Wotton		0794	46	16	1341187
Ockley	Park Cottage		PELLING	George	Lodg	U	28	M	Brickmaker	SUR	Ewhurst		0794	46	16	1341187
Ockley	Henhurst Cross	//	WHENHAM	Wm.	Head	M	39	M	Partner In Br+	SUS	East Grinstead		0794	46	16	1341187
Ockley	Henhurst Cross		WHENHAM	Anne	Wife	M	43	F	Wife	SUR	Capel		0794	46	16	1341187
Ockley	Henhurst Cross		WHENHAM	Charles	Son	U	13	M	Scholar	SUR	Capel		0794	46	16	1341187
Ockley	Henhurst Cross		WHENHAM	David	Son	U	10	M	Scholar	SUR	Capel		0794	46	16	1341187

+ = SEE ORIGINAL CENSUS FOR FULL DATA
M = MARRIED U = UNMARRIED W = WIDOW(ER) D = DIVORCED O = OTHER
m = MONTHS w = WEEKS d = DAYS > = GREATER THAN < = LESS THAN
N = SEE MISCELLANEOUS NOTES

As Enumerated fiche from 1881 Census Index

background information about the environment, but to detect married children living nearby.

The Pelling Family provides a good example of what can be learnt by doing this.

Alexander Pelling was not in Ockley on census night 1881 (see page 44) but the census entries for Park Cottage, Ockley contain a surprising amount of information about his family, not all of it apparent at first glance but obtainable with a little thought and detective work.

Two families are shown as sharing the cottage. The first consists of Edward Whenham, and his wife Ann, lately the widow of Michael Pelling who died in 1861 (her age and place of birth provide the clues), and her son Richard (son in law in the 19th century often means stepson and Richard was stepson to the head of the household). The second family comprises Michael's eldest daughter, Hannah, who married Mark Jenkins in Dorking Registration District in the December quarter of 1869, two of their children, and Hannah's brother, George, described as a lodger. Michael Pelling was listed as a beerhouse keeper in 1851 and as a labourer just before his death in 1861 but Edward Whenham is a partner in a brickyard and both his stepsons appear to have been taken into the family business.

The problem of illiteracy runs like a thread through all records and the census is no exception, spelling variants will again be found and ages cannot be relied upon. Some ladies appear to have found the secret of retaining their youth and age less than 10 years between censuses.

Often overlooked but valuable in finding out, for example, whether a Nonconformist chapel existed prior to 1851, is the Ecclesiastical Census for that year, held at the Public Record Office, Kew. Although purely voluntary, many places of worship made returns which show name, denomination, place, date of consecration or erection, space available for worship, the minister or other official, the estimated attendances on 30 March 1851 and the average attendances in the previous year (some figures appear wildly optimistic).

Wales

A complete set of census returns for Wales 1841-1891 is at the National Library of Wales, Aberystwyth SY23 2AZ.

Scotland

A complete set of census returns for Scotland 1841-1891 is at New Register House, Edinburgh (a charge is payable to search these). Most county libraries hold copies of the census returns for their own areas and there are a number of indexes in preparation. For the 1881 census see Chapter 7.

Ireland

Unfortunately, almost all Irish census returns up to 1851 were destroyed in 1922 and those for 1861 to 1891 were destroyed by government order. As compensation, the censuses for 1901 and 1911 may be consulted. These, together with the survivals from previous returns, for the whole of Ireland are at the National Archives in Dublin.

Channel Islands

A complete set of these returns 1841-1891 will be found at the Family Records Centre. Complete sets for the relevant islands are held on Jersey and Guernsey. The 1851 and 1891 censuses for Jersey have been indexed.

Isle of Man

Complete sets of these returns 1841-1891 will be found at the Family Records Centre and on the island. The 1851 census has been indexed.

The Genealogical Society of Utah,

50 East North Temple, Salt Lake City, Utah 84150, U.S.A. (the genealogical 'arm' of the Church of Jesus Christ of Latter-day Saints) holds copies on microfilm of all the publically available census returns for the British Isles. The Family History Centres of the LDS Church provide a service whereby any filmed census may be ordered for a small cost, which entitles you to view that reel at the FHC for between one and three months.

Bibliography

An Introduction to The Census Returns of England and Wales, Susan Lumas. FFHS, 1992.

Making Use of the Census, 3rd edition, Susan Lumas. P.R.O. Readers' Guide No.1, 1997.

Census Returns 1841-1891 on Microfilm: A Directory to Local Holdings, 6th edition, Jeremy Gibson. FFHS, 1994.

Marriage, Census and Other Indexes for Family Historians, 6th edition, Jeremy Gibson & Elizabeth Hampson. FFHS, 1996.

Local Census Listings 1522-1930, 3rd edition, Jeremy Gibson & Mervyn Medlycott. FFHS, 1994.

Pre-1841 Censuses and Population Listings, 4th edition, C.R. Chapman. Lochin Publishing, 1994.

Census Records for Scottish Families, Gordon Johnson. Aberdeen and North-East Scotland FHS, 1998. (164 King Street, Aberdeen AB24 5BD)

CHAPTER TEN

Parish Registers, Bishops' Transcripts and Marriage Licences

Parish Registers are books kept by the Established Church primarily to record baptisms/christenings, marriages and burials. All the countries within the British Isles maintained these, although they did not all commence at the same time or contain identical types of information. Bishops' Transcripts were kept only in England, Wales and the Isle of Man. Marriage Licences survive for England and Wales; indexes and abstracts for Ireland .

England and Wales

Early Registers and Bishops' Transcripts

The earliest Registers date from 1538 when Thomas Cromwell, Vicar General to Henry VIII, ordained that every marriage, christening and burial in the parish should be recorded. The entries were generally on paper and sixty years later, in 1598, an Act ordered that these Registers be copied onto parchment, but the wording was unfortunate. It said that entries from the old Registers should be copied 'but especially since the first year of Her Majesty's reign'. This gave the lazy an excuse to copy only from 1558 and that is why many Registers begin with that year. The 1598 Act approved a provincial constitution of Canterbury of 1597, which provided that, within a month after Easter, transcripts of the Registers for the previous year should be sent to the bishop in whose diocese the parish was situated. The earliest Bishops' Transcripts, therefore, date from 1597. Their survival rate varies greatly; always check the coverage as you work as some years will almost invariably be missing. With this in mind, it is worth noting that, for some counties, the IGI has been compiled from BTs and not PRs. When Civil Registration commenced in 1837, many incumbents ceased to send copies, especially of marriages, but some conscientious clergy continued to do so for some years afterwards. The importance of Bishops' Transcripts is that they provide a second record, which may have survived when the Parish Register has perished. Even if the Register exists the corresponding BT entry should be checked because it sometimes includes additional, or varying, information.

An unfortunate gap occurs in many Parish Registers during the period of the Civil War and Interregnum 1643-1660 and BTs do not survive for these years. Registers were often not properly maintained and the quality and completeness of the record (if any) varies considerably with the area.

The Calendar and the Dating System

The inexperienced searcher will find some dates in Registers baffling and a short digression is appropriate to consider the dating system, which is a fascinating study in itself. (See also page 35 and Bibliography to Chapter 6.)

Charles II left his exile in France on 5 June 1660 and landed at Dover on 25 May. Although having many claims to fame, time travel was not one of them and he could only achieve what at first appears a remarkable feat with the aid of the different calendars in use on the Continent and in England.

In England the (Old Style) Julian calendar was still in use whereas most of the Continent had adopted the (New Style) Gregorian calendar in 1582, as had Scotland in 1600. The Old Style calendar started the year on 25 March instead of 1 January. England had realised that it was 'out of step' which is why some Registers have 'double dating' with dates recorded as, for example, 22 February 1722/3 (i.e. 1722 Old Style, 1723 New Style).

The Julian calendar was, by 1751, incorrect by 11 days and Chesterfield's Act, passed in that year, decreed not only that the following 1 January should be the first day of 1752 but that 2 September that year should be followed the next day by 14 September. The effect for successive years was:

1750 commenced 25 March 1750 and ended 24 March 1750/1
1751 commenced 25 March 1751 and ended 31 December 1751
1752 commenced 1 January 1752 and ended 31 December 1752
(11 September days missing)

Bankers, however, refused to have their year truncated and the financial year due to finish on 25 March was extended by 11 days to 5 April. This anomalous Financial Year continues to this day as no Chancellor since has had the nerve to cut short one of his years.

Later Parish Registers

The next significant date is 25 March 1754 when Hardwicke's Marriage Act, passed the previous year, came into force. Its stated objective was 'An Act for the better prevention of clandestine (secret) marriages' and in this it was largely successful. Henceforth, all marriages had to be performed in the Parish Church or designated Parochial Chapelry, except for those involving Quakers and Jews, who were already keeping satisfactory records. It may surprise you to learn that prior to 1929 marriages could be contracted by boys from the age of 14 and girls from the age of 12. There had for many years been two ways to notify intention to marry, either by Licence or by the publication of Banns. However, many clergymen were lax and married persons from distant parishes, who had not resided in the cleric's parish for the requisite period, without a Licence or the calling of Banns.

Hardwicke's Act ordered that all marriages must be preceded by the calling of Banns or by the issuing of a Licence, that written parental consent was required by minors (under 21) for marriage by licence, and that registers of banns must be kept. The importance of the Banns Register should be realised. Occasionally information is given which is not in the Marriage Register and, where the bride and groom were of different parishes, the banns were read in both so that there is a record of intended marriages in other parishes, which might otherwise be difficult to find. Remember that banns denote an intention to marry; this does not mean that the marriage necessarily took place, though most did, and it is still necessary to trace the marriage entry.

In 1783 a Stamp Duty of three pence was imposed on every entry recorded in the Parish Register. Taxation is inevitably followed by evasion; paupers were exempted from the tax, and the number of 'paupers' recorded in the registers rose dramatically. Undoubtedly some people avoided the tax by not having their children baptised. The Act was repealed in 1794 and it is worth looking for several children of a family being baptised in a mass baptism after this date!

Rose's Act of 1812, effective from 1 January 1813, provided for separate registers to be kept for baptisms, marriages and burials respectively in specially printed books. The forms for baptism and burial have not changed to this day; those for marriage were altered in 1837 when civil registration began.

Information to be found in Parish Registers and Licences

Particularly prior to 1754, many register books are a hotch potch. Pages of baptisms may be interspersed with marriages and burials. Sometimes pages include details of all three types of event. The years covered for each event in the register may be different. Parchment was expensive so some ministers used minute writing and others would fill in any small spaces with events occurring several years later than most of those on the page. Until 1733 some registers were kept in Latin – see pages 34-35 for some of the words used, and their translation, which should enable you to understand these. Brief details of the information generally to be found in Parish Registers follow but you should look at the Bibliography to find books which will provide a much fuller picture of what you may be able to discover.

Baptisms

The information given varies greatly. In early registers you may find the simple entry of the name of the child, generally (but not always) followed by the name of the father. Some registers give the christian name of the mother in addition. The most helpful include the father's occupation; some include the precise place where the parents lived within the parish and sometimes the date of birth is stated. The majority of baptisms took place within a month of the birth but many took place months, or even years, later. Adult baptisms were not uncommon. Occasionally, particularly between 1770 and 1812 and mostly in the north of England, details of grand-parents are given.

After 1812, printed registers provide eight baptisms per page with columns for: child's christian name, christian names of parents, father's surname, father's occupation and place of residence, and by whom baptised.

Marriages

Before 1754 many marriage entries consist of the date and the names of the couple and nothing more; a few will merely state 'John Smith and his wife married'. From the early 1700s it will generally be stated whether the marriage was by banns or licence. Hardwicke's Act, effective from 25 March 1754, laid down certain criteria which should have been met when recording marriages but it was very loosely worded and the interpretation of it varied widely. Many parishes purchased printed books of forms (from printers who used their own judgement as to what should be included so that one book might have a space for the marital status of the couple, another might instead include the groom's occupation) but others continued to handwrite the entire entry. The entries were to be signed by both parties, two or more witnesses and the officiating minister. Those who were illiterate made their marks, although there is some evidence that a mark did not always indicate illiteracy and a signature did not always mean that a person could read and write. Girls who could write, marrying boys who could not, sometimes made their marks to avoid embarrassing their grooms and some people learnt how to write their names especially for the ceremony. Names of the witnesses can be important and should always be noted. These were often relatives and may provide a vital clue to family relationships. It is, however, as well to look at previous and succeeding entries as the parish clerk or churchwarden often acted as a 'professional witness' and, in some cases, signed pages of a printed register in advance!

Marriage Licences

The entry should state whether the marriage was by licence. If an ancestor of yours did obtain a licence to marry you may be fortunate and obtain further information.

The licence itself was presented to the parson and few survive, but the associated allegations, bonds and registers of licences kept in the issuing office are much more likely to be extant and many have been published. The allegation (in legal terms, an affidavit) was a sworn statement that Canon Law had been observed and that there was no legal impediment to the proposed marriage. Two bondsmen were then required to lodge securities (until 1823) that parents or guardians had, if necessary, given their consent and that there was no present or pending impediment. One bondsman was usually the groom and the other often a relative. The information required varied with the diocese but frequently included, in addition to the groom's and bride's names, their status (i.e. bachelor, widower, spinster or widow), ages (particularly of minors), occupations, places of residence and the church where the marriage was to be celebrated. If the Parish Register entry indicates marriage by licence a search should be made for the associated documentation, first consulting any indexes available. These should also be searched whenever difficulty is experienced in tracing a marriage. It is a mistake to assume that only the gentry obtained licences.

An example will illustrate both this and the value of licences better than description:

2 January 1829 Edmund **Hills**, Hartfield, labourer, bachelor, 20 (with consent of Wm. **Hills**, Hartfield, publican) and Mary Anne **Pelling**, West Hoathly, single woman, 20 (with consent of Thomas **Pelling**, West Hoathly, labourer, her father). To marry at West Hoathly.

Jeremy Gibson's book on ***Bishops' Transcripts and Marriage Licences*** (see Bibliography) shows, for each county, the years for which bonds and allegations are available, where located and whether published or indexed.

Burials

Until 1812, often the name only is given, perhaps with the addition of the name of the father in the case of an infant burial; absence of this additional data does not imply an adult burial.

Once again some registers, particularly after about 1770, are more informative and may give any or all of the following: age, place of residence, occupation and marital status, such as 'spinster' or 'widow of ...'.

In 1678 an Act passed to benefit the wool trade required that 'no corpse of any person (except those who shall die of the plague) shall be buried in any shirt, shift, sheet or shroud . . . other than what is made of sheep's wool only'. An affidavit had to be sworn to that effect and penalties were imposed for non-compliance. Most parishes put nothing in writing about this in their registers; some added 'affidavit sworn', or an abbreviation of the words, after the entry; a few kept separate registers to record burials in woollen. If a family preferred to bury the corpse in silk or flax (linen) they could pay the fine and do so and the register may record, as do those for Pocklington in Yorkshire in the 1720s, 'Notice given of no Affidavit brought for...'. The Act was not repealed until 1814, but the practice had fallen into disuse long before that date.

From 1813 there are eight entries per page with spaces for: name, abode, date of burial, age and officiating minister.

Copies of Registers and Indexes

Having read about the International Genealogical Index in Chapter 7 you will realise that this is by far the most important Index available to help you to locate baptisms and marriages in many parish registers.

Save yourself much time and trouble, before beginning your search, by finding out whether the Register has been printed or copied and, if so, for what period. If it has been it may also have been indexed and you will be able to extract all entries for the name(s) you want, readily and quickly. Parish Register Societies were established in some counties with the express purpose of transcribing and publishing registers and some of these, including those for Lancashire and Yorkshire, are still in operation today.

Many published works have concentrated, for obvious reasons, on the earliest records for a particular parish. A convenient stopping point for many was 1812, after which, as already described, the format in which the Registers were kept was altered. The period from 1813 to 1837 (when civil registration started) used to be less easy to research but many family history societies have concentrated on transcribing and publishing registers for this 'gap' period and the IGI tends to be strong on these years so the problem is a diminishing one.

Marriages are usually the most difficult area of research since many took place in the bride's parish, and her name will not be known. In the event of parental disapproval, or for some other reason, the marriage may not have taken place in either spouse's parish but elsewhere, theoretically after the required period of residential qualification.

One of the first genealogists to recognise the need for Marriage Indexes was Percival Boyd, who worked on an index for 30 years prior to his death in 1955, his aim being to include every marriage in Parish Registers from 1538 to 1837. His achievement, with aid from a dedicated band of helpers, of indexing perhaps 12%-15% of all marriages, with at least partial coverage for some 4,200 parishes, is remarkable. It is not surprising that the coverage of the index is variable from county to county ranging from almost 100% of Cornish parishes to only 4% in Staffordshire, and it should be noted that even if a parish is included in the index not all years are necessarily covered. The index is housed in the library of the Society of Genealogists but many county libraries and record offices hold copies of their own county sections.

Recognising the value of Boyd's work, other equally dedicated genealogists and societies have, in recent times, started to compile Marriage Indexes for counties or areas in which they are particularly interested. Fees for consulting these indexes are generally modest and the invariable rule is that applications must always be made by letter and be accompanied by a stamped addressed envelope. (It is unwise to assume the accuracy of printed or indexed data, nor does an index normally contain all details which can be found in the original record, which should always be consulted.) For information on indexes which are currently available, see Bibliography to Chapter 7.

Where are the Registers and What is the Cost of Research?

Until fairly recently a substantial number were held locally in the churches but the Parochial Registers and Records Measure 1978, amended by the Church of England (Miscellaneous Provisions) Measure 1992, has led to most Registers more than a hundred years old being deposited in Diocesan Record Offices. This is often, but not always, also the County Record Office. Deposited Registers can usually be studied free of charge.

Before undertaking a journey to a distant Parish there are a number of factors to consider, not least the potential cost. Incumbents and Parochial Church Councils still holding registers are legally obliged to permit access 'at all reasonable hours' but are entitled to charge fees to anyone wishing to search the registers (under the Ecclesiastical Fees Measure 1986); in 1998 the statutory charge for a 'particular search' (i.e. one made with a view to finding a specific entry and where the approximate date is known) for one hour is £12. The fee for a more general search is negotiable.

It should be emphasised that the scale of charges under this measure applies only to researches carried out in person. The incumbent is not obliged to permit the register (or any other record) to be photocopied or photographed or to make searches on behalf of an enquirer. If research is carried out in response to a postal enquiry, the incumbent is entitled to charge for time taken and is recommended to ask for payment in advance. Some parishes appoint a local archivist who will consult the registers for enquirers or be present whilst the searcher is looking at the records, again on payment of a fee.

Therefore, whether making a personal search or requesting information by post, it is prudent to ascertain how much you will be expected to pay and to negotiate a rate in advance.

Scotland

The Old Parish Registers (OPRs) – those earlier than 1855 – in Scotland were often badly kept. The majority date from the eighteenth century; a number survive for the seventeenth century, but few for the sixteenth. Deposited Registers are at New Register House, Edinburgh (see page 29 for details): a charge is made for consulting the Registers. One bonus is that where a baptism is recorded the mother's maiden name may be stated. Unfortunately there is a dearth of burial or death records, which in any case give little information. Due to this the enormous amount of work undertaken to record Monumental Inscriptions has great significance. The largest collection can be found at the Scottish Genealogy Society Library, 15 Victoria Terrace, Edinburgh, which also holds a wealth of material pertaining to Scottish family history and associated subjects.

The Church of Jesus Christ of Latter-day Saints has compiled a county by county index to the Old Parish Registers of baptisms and marriages: Miscellaneous Records have also been indexed. The indexes are available at New Register House, at Family History Centres, the Scottish Genealogy Society, and, in London, at the Family Records Centre and the Society of Genealogists. For Internet access see page 29.

Ireland

After the dis-establishment of the Church of Ireland in 1869, Acts of Parliament decreed that its registers were to be deposited at the Public Record Office in Dublin, which unfortunately was burned in the 'troubles' of 1922. Only four registers survived the holocaust but about one third had not been deposited and copies had been made of others. Church of Ireland registers (originals, transcripts or on microfilm) are in various locations. They may be in local custody; in the National Archives; in PRONI (mainly from Ulster); or in the Representative Church Body Library (for addresses see page 30). Details of Church of Ireland registers held in Dublin, with covering dates, are contained in John Grenham's ***Tracing your Irish Ancestors;*** check with the institutions mentioned for recent acquisitions.

Roman Catholic Registers, which mostly remain at the churches, are generally of later date, particularly for rural parishes; many do not begin until the nineteenth century and some do not commence until 1870. Microfilm copies of most pre-1880 registers are held at the National Library in Dublin.

All original Marriage Licence bonds were destroyed in 1922 but indexes, transcripts and abstracts survive; for details of availability see the Gibson Guide in the Bibliography.

The parish graveyard was often a common resting place for all denominations and burial entries may well be found in the registers of the Established Church. There are virtually no Roman Catholic burial registers. Presbyterian burial registers which survive are mostly from Ulster and copies are in PRONI.

Channel Islands

Jersey

The original registers are still in the charge of the parish rectors. Most are in French; the earliest (St Saviour) dates from 1540. All the registers are being indexed and copies are held by the Channel Islands FHS and in the Library of the Société Jersiaise. The latter also holds an indexed photocopy of the register for the garrison of Elizabeth Castle 1714-1817.

Guernsey

Parish Registers for Guernsey, Herm and Jethou are still held in the parishes. The Priaulx Library, Candie, St Peter Port, Guernsey specialises in Family History and has a comprehensive collection of parish registers on microfilm. Opening hours: Monday-Saturday 9.30 am- 5pm.

Isle of Man

The majority of Anglican Registers commence in the seventeenth century. The original registers were called into the General Registry and copied; copies are held here and at the Manx Library. Baptisms and marriages are included on the IGI. Indexes of burial registers and transcription of Monumental Inscriptions has been completed by the Isle of Man FHS.

Bibliography

An Introduction to Church Registers, Lilian Gibbens. FFHS, 1994.

Bishops' Transcripts and Marriage Licences, 4th edition, Jeremy Gibson. FFHS, 1997.

Basic Facts about Using Baptism Records for Family Historians, Pauline Litton. FFHS, 1996.

Basic Facts about Using Marriage Records for Family Historians, Pauline Litton and Colin Chapman. FFHS, 1996.

Basic Facts about Using Death and Burial Records for Family Historians, Lilian Gibbens. FFHS, 1997.

Marriage, Census and Other Indexes for Family Historians, 6th edition, Jeremy Gibson & Elizabeth Hampson. FFHS, 1996.

Marriage Laws, Rights, Records and Customs, Colin Chapman and Pauline Litton. Lochin Publishing, 1996.

Record Offices: How to Find Them, 7th edition, Jeremy Gibson and Pamela Peskett. FFHS, 1996.

The Phillimore Atlas and Index of Parish Registers, 2nd edition, ed. C.R. Humphery-Smith. Phillimore, 1995.

Individual County Maps published by Institute of Heraldic and Genealogical Studies: show date of commencement of Parish Registers and Probate Jurisdictions. (Northgate, Canterbury, Kent CT1 1BA)

See also Bibliography to chapter 11.

National Index of Parish Registers: (published by Society of Genealogists)

Vol. 1*		*General Sources of births, marriages and deaths, before 1837.* (Indexed in Vol. 3).
Vol. 4	Part 1	*Surrey,* 1990.
Vol. 5*		*The West Midlands: Gloucestershire, Herefordshire, Oxfordshire, Shropshire, Warwickshire and Worcestershire.*
Vol. 6	Part 1	*Staffordshire,* 2nd edition, 1992.
	Part 2	*Nottinghamshire,* 2nd edition, 1995.
	Part 3	*Leicestershire and Rutland,* 1995.
	Part 4	*Lincolnshire,* 1995.
	Part 5	*Derbyshire,* 1995
Vol. 7*		*Cambridgeshire, Norfolk and Suffolk.*
Vol. 8	Part 1.	*Berkshire,* 1989.
	Part 2	*Wiltshire,* 1992.
Vol. 9	Part 1.	*Bedfordshire and Huntingdonshire,* 1991.
	Part 2.	*Northamptonshire,* 1991.
	Part 3	*Buckinghamshire,* 1992.
	Part 4	*Essex,* 1993.
	Part 5	*London and Middlesex,* 1995
Vol. 10	Part 1.	*Cheshire,* 1995.
Vol. 11*	Part 1.	*North East England: Durham and Northumberland.*
Vol. 12*		*Sources for Scottish Genealogy and Family History,* 1970.
Vol. 13*		*Wales.*

* Out of print.

CHAPTER ELEVEN

The Parish Chest

The injunction of 1538 which ordered the keeping of Parish Registers in England and Wales also required that each parish should provide 'one sure coffer, with two locks and keys' in which the register book was to be kept. As time went on, all sorts of other documents connected with the running of the parish came to be stored in these Parish Chests (along with the church silver and communion plate). These records will usually be found today in CROs. What W.E.Tate describes in ***The Parish Chest*** as 'the intimate connection between the parish and the poor' can provide a rich source of information often unobtainable elsewhere and give, perhaps more than any other source, an insight into the way of life of our forebears. The nearest equivalent in Scotland to most of these records is Kirk Sessions records.

Poor Law: Settlement and Removal

Until the Poor Law Amendment Act of 1834 the relief of the poor was the responsibility of the Parish and many Acts were passed from 1388 onwards. Some of those which are most likely to have affected your ancestors are:

1601 Poor Law Act ordered that the churchwardens and two to four other substantial householders be nominated yearly as overseers, who were authorised to deal with the relief of the poor, funds being provided by levying a rate on the local inhabitants. They were to meet every month and were to keep records of their activities and of the money they dealt with. Where these have survived they can reveal fascinating facts.

1662 Act of Settlement said that every individual should have an official parish of settlement, which must make provision for maintaining the person or family if they should fall on hard times and need funding from the poor rate. Each parish was responsible for those having a legal settlement within it, which could be achieved in several ways, including birth, apprenticeship, a full year's work and wages or owning or renting property. Strangers could be removed by order of the Justices and anyone staying temporarily, for example for harvesting, had to have a certificate from his own Parish agreeing to take him back.

1697 Settlement Act stated that poor persons might enter any parish provided they possessed a settlement certificate saying that their home parish would be responsible for them if they became paupers (i.e. needed financial help). One of the most iniquitous provisions of this Act (not repealed until 1782) was that a pauper (and his wife and children) 'shall wear upon the shoulder ... a large Roman P together with the first letter of the name of the parish ...'.

An ancestor's misfortune can prove of great assistance to the family historian. The pauper was brought before a magistrate and examined about his origins, parentage, and previous occupations. At the CRO those Examination and Removal Orders which have survived should be listed under the parish of removal or with Quarter Sessions Records, which are themselves a rich source of genealogical information (see Chapter 14). Transcribing and indexing of these orders and of settlement certificates is progressing in various counties so do check with the relevant FHS or CRO.

1834 Poor Law Amendment Act

This removed responsibility for the poor from individual parishes. It brought groups of parishes together into Unions administered by Boards of Guardians of the Poor, each Union being obliged to provide a Workhouse for the 'impotent poor' – be they elderly, disabled, unmarried pregnant girls or poor children. Records in the nineteenth century often show payments by the Board to paupers to enable them to emigrate. The law relating to settlement was not substantially changed until 1876.

Poor Law Unions were established in Scotland by the 1845 Poor Law Amendment Act and in Ireland by the Irish Poor Law Act of 1838, followed by the 1847 Extension Act.

Other Parish Records

Overseers' Accounts may contain details of payment for rent, clothes, medical and funeral expenses for the poor, with the names of the recipients.

Churchwardens' Accounts cover a wide variety of expenditure and may include payments to the poor and details of bastardy.

Bastardy Allegations, Examinations and Bonds were common – no-one wanted to take responsibility for an unmarried mother and her child (who were likely to be dependent on parish relief) so overseers would go to great lengths to force the mother to name the father of the child (or a father for the child ...) and then make him legally responsible for paying for its birth and upkeep. The Child Protection Agency is nothing new!

Poor Rate Books contain details of those who paid rates and can prove to be a virtual census of the more prosperous parishioners. Note that in Scotland there was no compulsory poor rate and dependence was on voluntary contributions.

Jose Pelling (see page 22) was not baptised at Rudgwick and, until I could locate his baptism, his parents were unknown. He was, however, a farmer and thus liable to pay the Poor Rate. Working backwards and forwards through the Rate Book showed the farm passing successively from John to Mary, his widow, to Jose and then to Michael. It also showed that Jose took over his father-in-law's farm. Since the farms were named it was a simple matter to check their location on the Tithe map for the

Parish, which showed that the farms were adjacent, so Jose had married the girl next door. The map also indicated that there were Estate Papers, examination of which provided an unexpected bonus of detailed maps of each farm named and its acreage, plus the name and location of each field. This shows the value of researching the records of a Parish in depth; references were also found in both the Overseers' and Churchwardens' Accounts which shed much light upon the decline in the family's fortunes, as did entries in the Vestry Minutes. **Vestry Minutes** chronicle the administration of the Parish and may include, for example, Parish apprenticeships.

Parish Apprenticeships: completing an apprenticeship was one of the means by which a legal settlement could be obtained. Where parents could afford to pay, a child would be apprenticed by voluntary consent, generally until the age of 21. Where pauper children, or the children of vagrants, were concerned, the parish officers could compel parishioners/rate payers to take them as apprentices. In many cases they were 'bound' to learn husbandry or housewifery (which, in effect, meant being used as farm labourers or house servants from a very early age). With the coming of the Industrial Revolution, the practice developed of sending wagon-loads of pauper children from parishes in London and the south-east to work as 'apprentices' in the mills of Lancashire, Yorkshire and Derbyshire.

Miscellaneous: some ministers and parish officials treated their registers and the various account books almost as diaries, inserting comments on the weather, local gossip and local events. The Parish Register of Pocklington in Yorkshire records the burial in 1733 of 'Thomas Pelling of Burton Stather in Lincolnshire, commonly called the flying man, who was killed against the battlement of the choir, when coming down the rope from the steeple of this church.' Thomas was not a steeplejack but an acrobat, an 18th century Blondin, entertaining people on a Saturday afternoon.

Bibliography

The Parish Chest, 3rd edition, W.E.Tate. Phillimore, 1983.
Quarter Sessions Records for Family Historians: A Select List, 4th edition, Jeremy Gibson. FFHS, 1995.
An Introduction to Poor Law Documents Before 1834, Anne Cole. FFHS, 1993.
Poor Law Union Records, Jeremy Gibson et al. FFHS, 1993 and 1998.
Vol. 1 South East & East Anglia 2nd edition
Vol. 2 Midlands & Northern England
Vol. 3 South West England, Marches & Wales, 2nd edition
Vol. 4 Gazetteer of England & Wales, 2nd edition

CHAPTER TWELVE

Nonconformist Records (England)

Many people know that their ancestors were Nonconformists, which for the purposes of this chapter embraces all denominations other than the Established Church. Those who do not know must always bear the possibility in mind, particularly when researches in relevant Established Church records have not proved fruitful. Many families have a long tradition of Nonconformity; others flirted briefly with one of the denominations mentioned, often when a charismatic minister moved into the area.

Nonconformists do appear in Established Church records and the use of born (instead of baptised) and interred (instead of buried) may be an indication of Nonconformity but it cannot be denied that Nonconformist research may be more difficult. Minority faiths were often persecuted and even in more tolerant times restrictions were placed on their activities. The subject of Nonconformity is vast and only the briefest of mentions of the main denominations can be made here. Fuller details can be found in the books listed in the Chapter Bibliography; those with Nonconformist ancestors in Wales, Scotland and Ireland will need to study the books listed in Chapter 5.

Non-Parochial Registers

A commission was appointed in 1836 to consider the state and authenticity of non-parochial registers in England and Wales. It recommended that all records should be sent to the Registrar General and many were surrendered at that time. The Catholics refused initially, as did the Society of Friends (Quakers), but both did deposit Registers following the Non-Parochial Registers Act in 1840, although the few Roman Catholic ones were almost all from north-east England. Dr Williams' Library surrendered an important register of births which was commenced in 1742 by a combined body representing Presbyterians, Congregationalists/Independents and Baptists (often known as 'the Three Denominations'), after concern had been expressed at the failure of many congregations to keep proper records. All these deposited non-parochial registers have now been transferred to the Public Record Office and are available on microfilm both at Kew and at the Family Records Centre; some which were deposited later are available only at Kew. Many CROs and libraries hold copies of the registers for their own counties and those deposited to 1840 are included in the IGI (see Chapter 7). Later registers may be found in CROs, with denominational historical societies, or still held at the local place of worship.

The importance of Hardwicke's Marriage Act has already been stressed. Between 1754 and 1837 all marriages, except for those of Quakers and Jews, had to be celebrated in an Anglican Church in order to be considered valid and the offspring legitimate. Between 1837 and 1899 marriages could be performed in a Nonconformist chapel if it was licensed and a Registrar was present to keep the official records.The chapel record was optional and not always kept; the official record will be found at the local Register Office. Following the 1898 Marriages Act, Nonconformist congregations were permitted to appoint an 'authorised person' to register marriages so the presence of the Registrar was no longer required.

Monumental Inscriptions.

These are very important to Nonconformist researchers since they may be the only records available. Anglican clergymen were not obliged to permit the burial of non-communicants in their churchyards, and burial grounds which catered for Nonconformists were established from the seventeenth century. The best known is probably that at Bunhill Fields in London, which was opened in 1665 (an index to the inscriptions is available in Guildhall Library). In Ireland, Clifton Graveyard in Belfast and in Scotland, Calton Hill Cemetery in Edinburgh were both opened in the 1770s. Many nineteenth century cemeteries contain non-denominational sections.

Roman Catholics

Many Roman Catholic records are still held by priests at the churches although an increasing number are being deposited in record offices and the Catholic Record Society has published much valuable material. Some record offices are presently surveying, and listing, all the records in their areas so do remember to ask what is available and where. Only 79 Catholic Registers were deposited in 1840 (many more have been handed in since), of which 46 were from Yorkshire, 12 from Durham and 10 from Northumberland. In Lancashire only one out of 71 known registers was deposited and there were none at all from 16 counties.

There is a Catholic Family History Society, which is a member of the FFHS. Details of Catholic Missions and surviving Registers 1700-1880 can be found in the series listed in the Bibliography.

Quakers (Society of Friends)

The Quakers, founded by George Fox in the mid-17th century, were the most record-conscious of all the Nonconformists. Before finally handing over all their registers – 1445 in 1840 and a further 121 in 1857 – digests (abstracts **not** transcripts) were made of the entries, some of which date from the 1600s. To give some idea of numbers, they include approximately 260,000 births (not baptisms). A complete set of these digests is kept at the Library of the Society of Friends, Friends House, Euston Road, London NW1 2BJ. They have been microfilmed and county sections may be available in libraries and record offices. A duplicate set of its own digests was made for each

Quarterly Meeting; details of their locations are given in ***My Ancestors were Quakers***, which also includes limited information on records in Wales, Ireland and Scotland.

The Quakers forbade marriage with non-Quakers and there was a very strict ban on cousin relationships. These strictures led to exhaustive enquiries about proposed marriages, for all of which, irrespective of the age of the parties, parental consent was required until 1883. The standard marriage certificate used from 1677 sometimes had as many as 40 witnesses (note that these are not included in the digests). Bear in mind that Quakers were not required to comply with Hardwicke's Marriage Act of 1753.

Quakers, in common with certain other denominations, refused to acknowledge months or days of the week named after heathen gods and used an alternative dating system consisting of numbers. This can cause problems for researchers, particularly in records up to 1752 before which date the New Year officially began on 25 March (see page 64).

For example: 25 March 1737 would be written as 'the twentyfifth day of the first month, 1737' and 31 Dec 1737 would be written as 'the thirty first day of the tenth month, 1737'. From 1752 January was accepted as the first month so the same dates in 1773 would read as 'the twenty fifth day of the third month, 1773' and 'the thirtyfirst day of the twelfth month, 1773'. A more detailed explanation can be found in the book mentioned above.

Jews

The Jews were originally expelled from England in 1290. Two principal groups have migrated to Great Britain since the 17th century:

(i) Sephardic – from Spain, Portugal and Italy.
(ii) Ashkenazi – from Eastern Europe, Bohemia, Germany and Holland.

They have settled quite widely throughout Britain, especially in the larger towns and cities, where synagogues were established, and their numbers increased rapidly in the late 19th and early 20th centuries. Jews were exempted from Hardwicke's Marriage Act of 1753. Useful addresses, bibliographies and other information will be found in ***My Ancestors were Jewish.***

United Reformed Church.

This was formed in 1972 by a union between the Congregational Church of England and Wales and the Presbyterian Church of England but note that not all Congregations accepted this union. The union led to a merger of the Presbyterian Historical Society of England and the Congregational Historical Society to form the United Reformed Church Historical Society, 86 Tavistock Place, London WC1H 9RT. Write in advance of a prospective visit as the library is only open on certain days.

(i) **Congregationalists (also called Independents)**
No less than 1,278 chapels surrendered Registers in 1840, Yorkshire providing 138, more than twice the total for any other county apart from London's 77. A number of Congregations did not accept the 1972 union and there are several smaller Federations. Details of these, with addresses, together with a 'hopefully exhaustive gazetteer of chapels in England and Wales [founded before 1850]', listing surviving registers and their present whereabouts, can be found in ***My Ancestors were Congregationalists in England and Wales***.

(ii) **Presbyterians and Unitarians**
194 Presbyterian and 6 Unitarian registers were deposited. Lancashire was the leading county with 29 (and 2), nearly double that of the next county Yorkshire 15 (and 3). Details can be found in ***My Ancestors were English Presbyterians/Unitarians***, which also includes listings of Presbyterian Congregations in Scotland and Ireland.

Baptists

Bear in mind that Baptists do not favour infant baptism but often registered the births of their children. 431 chapels in England and Wales (Yorkshire again having the largest number) surrendered registers in 1840, of which there is a complete list in the book ***My Ancestors were Baptists.***

Methodists

It was not the wish of John Wesley (1703-1791) to separate from the Church of England and during his lifetime Methodist Chapels were called 'Preaching Houses', the parish church being used for baptisms, marriages and burials. A few registers date from the 1790s, when baptisms commenced in some chapels and burial grounds were also established; the greater number begin between 1810 and 1820. Following Wesley's death a number of schisms occurred and the problem often is to identify to which splinter group a particular chapel or an ancestor belonged. Details of the various secessions will be found in ***My Ancestors were Methodists.*** When exploring Methodist records it should be remembered that a man who was, say in 1840, a strong member of the Methodist New Connexion, could have started life as a Wesleyan and been baptised and perhaps married at a completely different chapel.

Following the Acts in 1840 and 1858, 856 Methodist registers were deposited. Yorkshire again led the field with those surrendered in 1840: 138 Wesleyan Methodist registers, 17 Primitive Methodist and 15 Methodist New Connexion. Cornwall, with 11, headed the list of **Bible Christian** registers handed in. This group was established in the west country in 1815 and was the only one of those seceding not to include the word 'Methodist' in its name.

Bibliography

National Index of Parish Registers:

Vol. 2* Sources for Nonconformist Genealogy and Family History, D.J.Steel. Society of Genealogists, 1973.

Vol. 3* Sources for Roman Catholic and Jewish Genealogy and Family History, D.J.Steel & E.R.Samuel. Society of Genealogists, 1974.

Basic Facts about English Nonconformity, Michael Gandy. FFHS, 1998.

Sources for the History of English Nonconformity 1660-1830, Michael Mullett. British Records Association, 1991.

Catholic Missions and Registers 1700-1880, Michael Gandy (author and publisher), 1993.

- ***Volume 1 London and the Home Counties***
- ***Volume 2 Midlands and East Anglia***
- ***Volume 3 Wales and the West of England***
- ***Volume 4 North East England***
- ***Volume 5 North West England***
- ***Volume 6 Scotland***

My Ancestors were: How can I find out more about them? series. Published by the Society of Genealogists.

- ***My Ancestors Were Quakers,*** E.H.Milligan and M.J.Thomas. 1990.
- ***My Ancestors Were Jewish,*** 2nd edition, Isobel Mordy. 1995.
- ***My Ancestors Were Congregationalists in England and Wales,*** D.J.H.Clifford. 1992.
- ***My Ancestors Were English Presbyterians/Unitarians,*** Alan Ruston. 1993.
- ***My Ancestors Were Baptists,*** 3rd edition, Geoffrey R. Breed. 1995.
- ***My Ancestors Were Methodists***, 2nd edition, William Leary. 1993.
- ***My Ancestors Were In The Salvation Army,*** Ray Wiggins. 1997.

* Out of print.

CHAPTER THIRTEEN

Wills, Letters of Administration and Inventories

'Where there's a will there's a way', is often said in a different context, implying that if you have the determination you will succeed and, genealogically speaking, it is very apt.

Wills are the truest and most reliable genealogical record available and yet probably the least used. In some cases they are the only firm way of establishing family relationships where two persons of the same name lived in the same neighbourhood at the same time. No-one can say exactly what percentage of people in the past made Wills but don't make the mistake of believing that only the rich did so. You will find that people whom you would expect to leave a Will either didn't, because they died before they found the time to make one, or did but the family never took it to probate because that cost money and there was no argument over how the effects were to be divided so there is no record of it. Equally, you will find that some farm labourers left documents meticulously dividing their few possessions.

If poor law material can provide a clear insight into the lives our ancestors led, Wills give an unrivalled glimpse into their minds and the minutiæ of every day living. Anne Lytton, dying in Derbyshire in 1688, left to her son George, who lived about five miles away, 'one cow by the name of Throstle' and to her daughter Jane 'one pair of sheets'. Moses Longden, dying in the same county in 1764, and making one of his daughters 'execeter of this my last will and testiment', provided for his widow and then added 'All so i apoint my children every [one of them] a whomestid [homestead] till they are provided for, that is to say when are sick or sore or out of place'.

We are all familiar with the phrase 'last Will and Testament' but a question seldom asked is, what is the difference? The answer is simple, a Will was concerned with realty (real estate) and a Testament with personalty (personal property). Scotland used the word testament for the records confirming an estate's executors, whether or not there was a Will, but it must be appreciated that Scottish (Roman) Law is different from the English system. In Scotland a man could only freely dispose of his estate if his wife and children did not survive him, otherwise he could only dispose of part of it as he chose; the rest was bequeathed according to set rules. The same system had originally applied in England but it was gradually eroded and virtually ceased to apply by the end of the seventeenth century.

The Statute of Wills 1540 provided that Wills could be made by boys from the age of 14 and girls from the age of 12. These ages applied until 1837 in England and Wales. A valid Will could be made by almost anyone apart from children, lunatics, convicted traitors and felons, and married women. A married woman could not make a Will without her husband's consent until the Married Women's Property Act of 1882. An English Will is revoked by a subsequent marriage, a Scottish Will is not. Until 1837 a Holograph Will, entirely in the deceased's handwriting, did not require witnesses (and, in some circumstances, is still recognised as valid in Scotland). Nuncupative (oral) Wills were valid if there were witnesses; but after 1837 they were only acceptable from military or naval personnel on active service.

A Will names a person or persons, the executor(s) (a woman is an executrix), to carry out the deceased's (testator or testatrix) wishes. The executor has to obtain an official document from the Court, the grant of probate, to prove he is the person legally authorised to administer the estate. If the deceased did not make a Will then he is said to have died intestate and Letters of Administration (usually abbreviated to Admon.) must be obtained by the next of kin. Sometimes Letters of Administration are granted even when there is a Will because the executor has died or declined to act.

England and Wales

From 11 January 1858, civil District Probate Registries were opened, and replaced the Ecclesiastical Courts system described below. Copies of all Wills proved and Letters of Administration granted subsequent to this date are held by the Principal Registry of the Family Division; DPRs may hold original Wills proved in their areas. Annual consolidated indexes were printed and, from mid-1998, these may be consulted in the public search room at First Avenue House, 42-48 High Holborn, London WC1V 6HA (having previously been available at Somerset House). Check before visiting. These indexes are really abstracts and contain information concerning date and place of death, principal beneficiaries and the value of the estate. They can often be used as a short cut to find the date of death for most men of substance dying after 1857. Each District Probate Registry received an annual set of these indexes (to 1928 or later) most of which have been transferred to county record offices or major libraries, locations being given in ***Probate Jurisdictions*** (see Bibliography).The indexes have also been microfiched to 1935 and are becoming more widely available so always check locally. A set can be found on the first floor of the Family Records Centre. Copies of Wills and Admons. should be ordered from the Probate Registry, Duncombe Place, York, YO1 2EA (Tel. 01904 624210), giving full name, date of death and last address of the testator. The cost is currently £2 (cheques payable to HM Paymaster General) and allow 28 days for delivery.

Prior to 1858 Wills in England had to be proved in the Ecclesiastical Courts (of which there were some 300) and it is the complex system of these which most people find confusing because of the difficulty of determining which Court had jurisdiction. The searcher will often not know the reason why a Will was proved in a particular Court and all should be searched in the order shown in the flow chart on the next page.

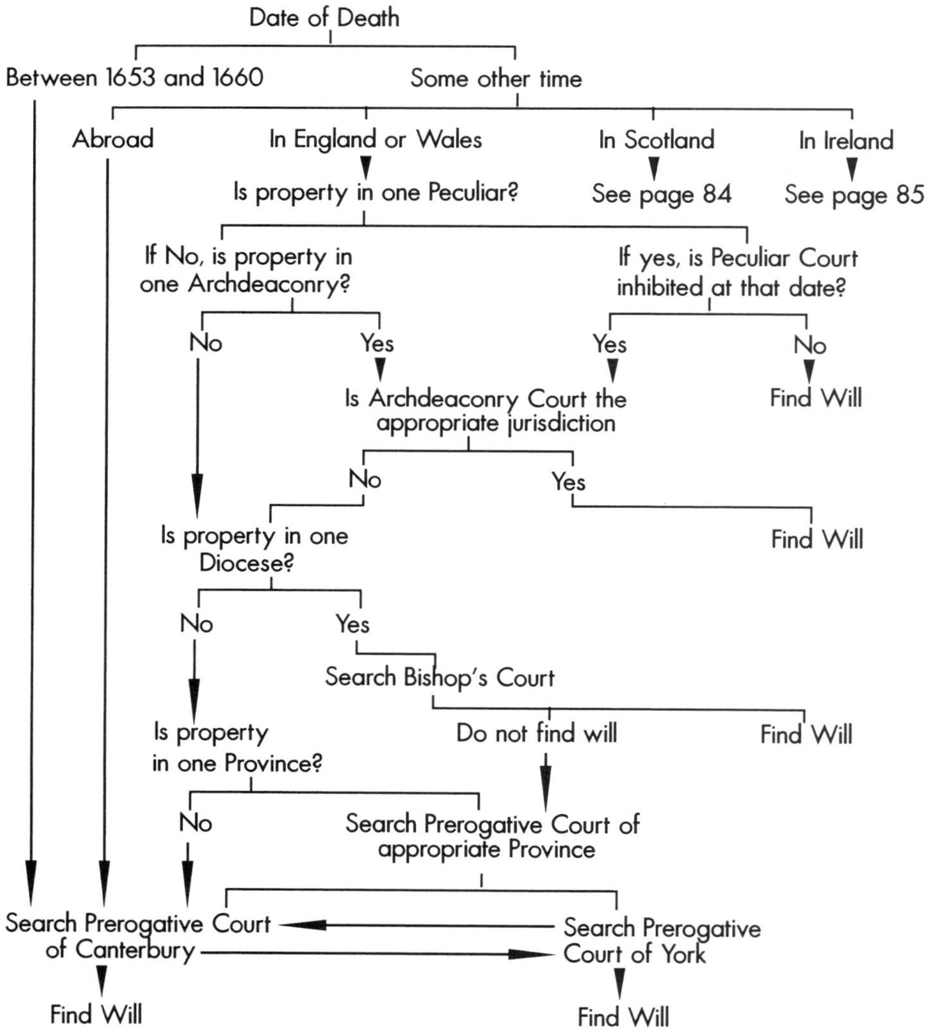

Finding the appropriate ecclesiastical probate court

Organisation of the Church of England

The status of an Ecclesiastical Court is related to church administration which is as follows:

The **Parish** is the smallest unit, having a vicar or rector or perpetual curate and then:

(a) **Rural Deanery:** an area consisting of a number of parishes (not usually more than 12) headed by a rural dean who is usually minister of one of its parishes.

(b) **Archdeaconry:** consists of a number of rural deaneries each in the charge of an archdeacon.

(c) **Diocese:** consists of several archdeaconries over which a bishop has authority.

(d) **Province:** a large area of several Dioceses with the authority vested in an Archbishop. Until the Archbishopric of Wales was created in 1920 there were only two (Canterbury and York).

(e) **Peculiar:** an area which, by ancient custom, was exempt from the Archdeacon's, and often the Bishop's, authority. It might consist of a single parish; several parishes, either adjacent or widely separated, possibly even in different counties; a Manorial Court; a University or a College (Oxford and Cambridge); certain cities and towns.

Probate Jurisdiction

The Courts of Jurisdiction can now be considered, bearing the above hierarchy in mind.

(a) **Rural Deans:** did not normally exercise probate jurisdiction in the Province of Canterbury but in the Province of York it was customary for them to do so under commission from the Bishop.

(b) **Archdeacon's Court:** if property was held solely within one Archdeaconry in the Province of Canterbury and if the Archdeaconry exercised its jurisdiction (the Bishop claimed jurisdiction over those which did not), then normally the Will was proved in this Court.

(c) **Bishop's Diocesan or Consistory (Commissary) Court:** granted probate where property was held in more than one archdeaconry within the same diocese.

(d) **Archbishop's Court:** granted probate where property was held in more than one diocese. There were two courts:
The Prerogative Court of Canterbury (PCC) covered most counties.
The Prerogative Court of York (PCY) covered Cheshire, Cumberland, Durham, Isle of Man, Lancashire, Northumberland, Nottinghamshire, Westmorland and Yorkshire.

(e) **Peculiars.** These were the smallest probate divisions. Their number varied from county to county - Yorkshire had more than 50 peculiar jurisdictions whereas Cheshire had none.

At times Peculiar Courts were inhibited (i.e. closed) in which case the next superior Court exercised jurisdiction. Wills were normally proved in Peculiar Courts if the deceased's property was solely within that Peculiar.

If property was held in both provinces or outside England then Canterbury claimed superior jurisdiction. PCC also had jurisdiction over the estates of those who died overseas. Moreover, executors of people of standing often used a higher court than was necessary. In the period 1653-1660 almost all Wills were proved in the PCC.

PCC Wills are held at the Public Record Office and may be consulted on microfilm there or at the Family Records Centre. Indexes to the Wills 1383-1700 and 1750-1800 have been published; there is a typescript consolidated index for the period 1701-1749 at both repositories and yearly manuscript calendars for the period 1801-1852. PCY Wills are at The Borthwick Institute of Historical Research, St Anthony's Hall, Peasholme Green, York YO1 2PW. Other Wills are to be found in various repositories. ***Probate Jurisdictions*** sets out in detail where the Wills for each county in England and Wales are to be found.

Death Duty or Estate Duty Registers

These date from 1796, when a Legacy Duty was first imposed, and are held at the PRO. The indexes 1796-1903 (and some Registers) are available on microfilm at the PRO or the FRC; SoG has copies of indexes to 1858. For further information see Jane Cox's books in the Bibliographies to this chapter and to Chapter 5.

Scotland

Some differences in Scottish law have already been mentioned. Until 1868 only moveable property could be bequeathed by Will. After the Reformation the function of confirming testaments in Scotland (previously exercised by the bishops' courts) was assumed by Commissary Courts set up by royal authority (1566); that of Edinburgh had a local and a national jurisdiction, and the right to confirm the testaments of persons dying out of Scotland but having moveable estate in the country. The jurisdictions of the lesser Commissary Courts covered areas with boundaries roughly the same as the mediaeval dioceses. From 1824 the function of confirming testaments was invested in the Sheriff Courts, although the Commissary Court of Edinburgh retained a local jurisdiction until 1830.

The records of most Sheriff Courts, including their extant commissary records, pass to the Scottish Record Office approximately ten to fifteen years after creation. The Office will advise you if records are still in the custody of the appropriate sheriff clerks. Indexes available in the SRO's search rooms in Edinburgh include those to the Commissary Courts' Registers of Testaments to 1800, published by the

Scottish Record Society (also available in many good reference libraries); indexes to the personal estates of defuncts, 1827-67 (covering dates varying for different sheriffdoms), which indicate the existence of a confirmed testament in the appropriate Sheriff Court records; certain internal indexes to registers of inventories and confirmations post 1823, transmitted to the SRO with Sheriff Court Records; the Calendar of Confirmations from 1876 to date. Extracts can usually be seen and copied but to view full entries the documents will need to be ordered in advance as they have to be brought in from outside repositories.

Ireland

Irish Wills were proved in diocesan courts from 1536 to 1858 (there were no archdeacons' courts), the Prerogative Court being that of the Archbishop of Armagh. Almost all original Wills were destroyed in 1922. However indexes to Diocesan Wills and Admons, and Prerogative Wills, are available in the Reading Room of the National Archives in Dublin. Various collections of transcripts and abstracts are held in the National Archives and elsewhere, including Betham's abstracts from pre-1800 Prerogative Wills and Admons. After 1858 annual indexes, containing identical details to those described for England on page 81, are on open access at the National Archives in Dublin and the Public Record Office of Northern Ireland in Belfast. Most twentieth century Wills, and Will Books from 1858 for many of the District Registries, but not for the principal Registry, are available in the same repositories.

Wales

In Wales, Wills were normally proved in the appropriate diocesan court, with recourse if needed to the PCC or PCY. Virtually all locally proved Welsh Wills prior to 1858 are at the National Library of Wales, Aberystwyth, as are post-1858 registered copy Wills for all Wales except Montgomeryshire.

Isle of Man

Locally proved probate material is still held on the Island. The Isle of Man was in the Province of York (Diocese of Sodor and Man).

Channel Islands

Locally proved probate material is still held on the Islands. The Channel Islands were in the Province of Canterbury (Diocese of Winchester but always administered separately).

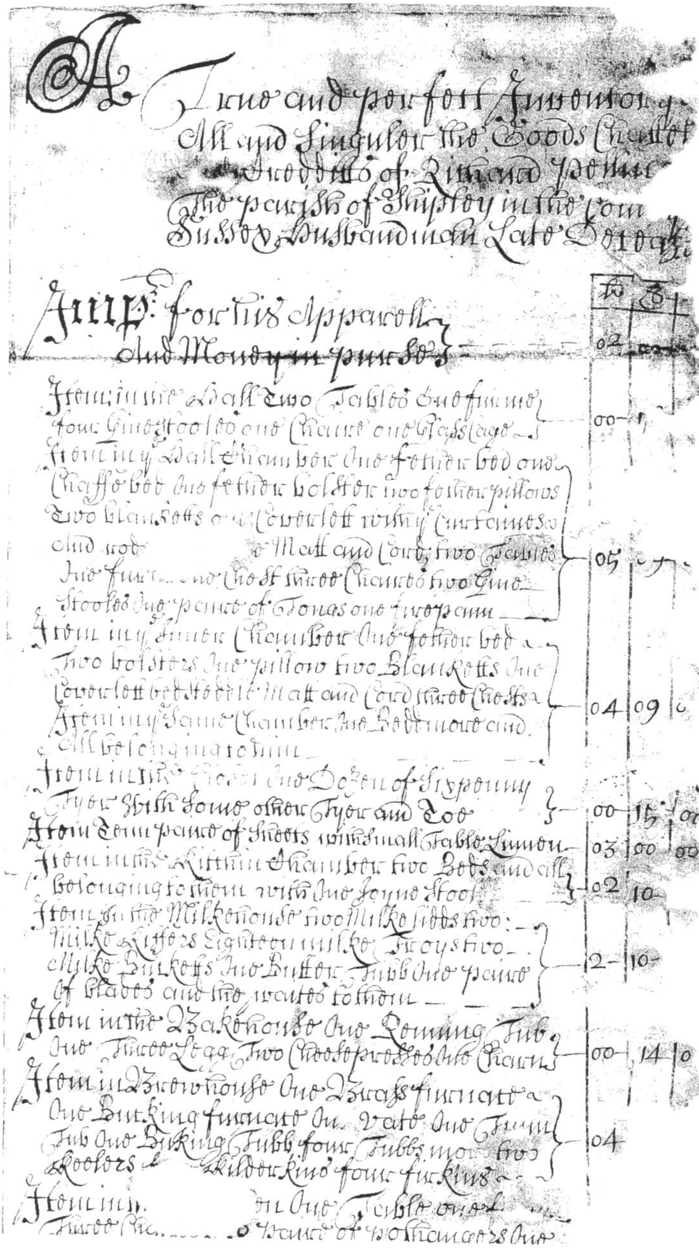
A True and perfect Inventory [of] All and Singular the Goods Chattels [and] Creditts of Richard [illegible] [of] The parish of Shipley in the County [of] Sussex Husbandman Late Deceased

Imp^s for his Apparell and Money in purse — 02

Part of an eighteenth century inventory

Inventories

Until the middle of the eighteenth century, as part of the process of obtaining probate or administration, several persons were usually appointed to take a true and perfect inventory of the personal estate of the deceased (a list of their belongings). The practice officially continued until 1782 but dropped off markedly after the 1750s, except in peculiars where it sometimes continued into the nineteenth century. Copies are normally available, with the probate or administration documents, in the appropriate record repository. Each should have included all goods moveable and immoveable; clothes, wares, leases, farm stock, cut grass and timber, growing corn, cash rent and debts due. Excluded were lands, inheritable property, and a wife's paraphernalia (personal belongings, such as clothes, which the law allowed a married woman to keep and treat as her own). PCC inventories survive only between 1661 and about 1720.

In many counties the inventory was listed room by room; an example from 1718 is illustrated and you will quickly realise that no other source is likely to give you such an insight into how your ancestors lived. You may think that you cannot read the example shown, but if you study it for a while you will see that it is: 'A true and perfect Inventory [of] All and Singular the Goods Chattels and Creddits of Richard Pellin, [of] The Parish of Shipley in the Cou[nty of] Sussex husbandman Late Deceas[ed]. The inventory begins 'Imp. [imprimis: firstly] for his Apparell And Money in purse £2.0.0' and continues with a list of the contents of every room, each one beginning with 'Item'. The first room reads 'Item in the Hall Two Tables one furme [form] four Gine stooles [joint stools] one Chaire one Glass Cage ...'; given this start I am sure you will be able to decipher most of it.

Bibliography

An Introduction to Wills, Probate and Death Duty Records, Jane Cox. FFHS, 1993.

A Simplified Guide to Probate Jurisdictions: Where to Look for Wills, 4th edition, Jeremy Gibson. FFHS, 1997. (Includes maps; covers whole of British Isles).

The Phillimore Atlas and Index of Parish Registers ed. C.R. Humphery-Smith. 2nd edition. 1995 – also shows probate jurisdictions.

Prerogative Court of Canterbury Wills and other Probate Records, Miriam Scott. PRO Readers' Guide 15.

See also Bibliographies to Chapters 5 and 10.

CHAPTER FOURTEEN

Other Useful Sources

Most of the documents described in the previous chapters will provide names, dates and (some) addresses, which should enable you to discover a great deal about your family history. There are, however, many, many more sources in which members of your family may be mentioned and a few of them are suggested here, with a Bibliography attached to each section. It is always worth checking with a local record office as to whether they have published guides to their own holdings of any of these records.

Heraldry

Some people begin their family history researches in the belief that they have a 'family coat of arms'. The current trend for commercial firms to produce everything from plaques to key-rings bearing these devices reinforces this belief but many people will be disappointed. Heraldry can be very useful to family historians – as well as being a fascinating study in its own right – but bear in mind that, with very few exceptions, the right to bear arms is granted to an individual and his direct descendants in the male line and not to all members of a family. It is unlikely that you will suddenly find yourself entitled to bear arms but if you can establish a link with an armigerous family you may well be able to link into one of the many published sources mentioned in Chapter 4.

Basic Facts about Heraldry for Family Historians, Iain Swinnerton. FFHS, 1995.
The Observer's Book of Heraldry, Charles MacKinnon, 1966.

Armed Services

If your family has a tradition of service in the army or the navy you may well be able to trace several generations through extensive records held mainly in the PRO at Kew (Chapter 5). Remember that the British Army has always contained a high proportion of Irish and Scottish soldiers. Bear in mind that, if searching before 1873 (army) or 1853 (navy), you really need to know in which regiment or ship your ancestor served. Records relating to the First World War are still in the process of being released for public study: officers' records were released early in 1998. If a family member was killed in either World War, it is well worth contacting the Commonwealth War Graves Commission (2 Marlow Road, Maidenhead, Berkshire SL6 7DX) to ask where they are commemorated (a nominal charge may be made).

If your ancestor did not serve in the regular forces, he may well have served in the militia or at least have been listed as being eligible to do so.

Don't forget the Royal Marines, the Merchant Navy, the fishing fleets and (in the 20th century) the Royal Air Force.

An Introduction to The British Army: Its History, Tradition & Records, Iain Swinnerton. FFHS, 1996.

My Ancestor was in the British Army: how can I find out more about him?, M.J. & C.T. Watts. Society of Genealogists, 1995.

World War One Army Ancestry, 3rd edition, Norman Holding. FFHS, 1997.

Naval Records for Genealogists, N.A.M.Rodger. HMSO, 1988 [out of print: new edition due 1998]

My Ancestor was a Merchant Seaman: how can I find out more about him?, M.J. & C.T. Watts. SoG, 1991.

Records of the Royal Marines, Garth Thomas. PRO, 1994.

Records of the Royal Air Force, Eunice Wilson. FFHS, 1991

Tudor and Stuart Muster Rolls, Jeremy Gibson & Alan Dell. FFHS, 1991

Militia Lists and Musters (1757-1876), 3rd edition, Jeremy Gibson & Mervyn Medlicott. FFHS, 1994.

Directories and Gazetteers

Libraries and some record offices usually have a good collection of these covering their locality.

Local Directories: were published from about 1780. Generally, a history and topographical description of the district is given and prominent persons and tradesmen are listed. The advertisements are particularly interesting, giving a true flavour of the period.

Gazetteers or Topographical Dictionaries: these may cover a county, a country or the British Isles and should list all places within that area, however small. County ones will usually say in which parish and local government area a place is situated.

Kelly's is the best known series of local directories.

Bartholomew's Gazetteers are recommended for wider coverage: those published before 1974 are of most value to family historians as they use the historic counties.

Newspapers

Having found the date of a birth, marriage or death, a check of the local paper may reveal more details; an obituary notice may contain a potted biography; the report of the funeral may include details of relatives. Even if the event is not recorded you will find out which items were making the news, and which may have influenced your ancestors' lives or environment. The most comprehensive collection of national and other newspapers (including foreign and commonwealth ones) is held by the British Library Newspaper Library (see Chapter 5). Provincial newspapers only began to include local news from the mid-18th century; before this they printed national and international news culled from London papers. Local newspapers proliferated from the mid-19th century.

An Introduction to Using Newspapers & Periodicals, C.R.Chapman. FFHS, revised 1996. (Includes useful bibliography.)

Local Newspapers 1750-1920 (England, Wales, Channel Islands, Isle of Man), Jeremy Gibson. FFHS, 1991. [Out of print: new edition pending.]

School and University Records

Schools' records may be found at local Record Offices although some schools still retain them. Lists of pupils for many of the Public Schools have been printed; the Society of Genealogists has a large collection of these. Extensive biographical details are often included in these and in the printed ***Alumni*** for the older universities (Oxford & Cambridge; St Andrew's, Glasgow, Aberdeen & Edinburgh; Trinity College, Dublin). It may be possible to trace several generations where, as often happened, sons of succeeding generations attended the same school or university.

The Growth of British Education & its Records, C.R.Chapman. Lochin Publishing, 1991.

Registers of the Universities, Colleges & Schools of Great Britain & Ireland, P. Jacobs. Athlone Press, 1964.

Children's Societies

Many children, particularly in the late 19th and early 20th centuries, became the responsibility of children's homes and the children's societies and a number were sent overseas, mainly to Canada and Australia. Some addresses and suggested reading are given in ***The Family Historian's Enquire Within.*** Thousands also passed through the Foundling Hospital from its foundation in 1739 (now the Thomas Coram Foundation; its records are held by the London Metropolitan Archives).

Taxation

Our ancestors suffered, as we do, from the need of government to finance its activities. The most useful 18th and 19th century tax lists for the family historian are those for the **Land Tax**. Although this was collected from the 1690s, most of the surviving records (in county record offices) are for the period 1780 to 1832, when payment of the tax was a voting qualification. Names of owners of land and their tenants are given, annually, though occupants of cottages are often un-named. Virtually no records survive for Scotland. In Ireland, Griffith's Valuation (1846-1865) lists landowners and tenants.

Records of the **Hearth Tax**, listing virtually all heads of households (with the number of fireplaces, or heated rooms, in their homes), giving occupiers rather than owners, may survive between 1662 and 1674 for England and Wales; 1691 for Scotland.

This tax was succeeded by the **Window Tax** from 1696 to 1851; far fewer records survive for England and Wales; the Scottish Record Office has an extensive collection covering 1748-1802.

Land and Window Tax Assessments, Jeremy Gibson, Mervyn Medlycott & Dennis Mills. FFHS, 1993.

The Hearth Tax, other Later Stuart Tax Lists and the Association Oath Rolls, 2nd edition, Jeremy Gibson. FFHS, 1996.

The Local Historian's Encyclopaedia, 2nd edition, John Richardson. Historical Publications, 1986. Contains a useful section listing taxes & dates and another dealing with Land Records.

Land Records

Your ancestors may not have been land owners but many of them will have been land occupiers (tenants).

If they did inherit or purchase land (and that includes houses) and lived in Middlesex, Yorkshire or Ireland you are fortunate because **Deeds Registries** existed here from the early 1700s and most sales or transfers of land are recorded. Middlesex records are in London Metropolitan Archives, 40 Northampton Road, Clerkenwell, London EC1R 0HB; those for Ireland are in Dublin (see page 30) and for Yorkshire in the record offices in Beverley (East Riding); Northallerton (North Riding); Wakefield (West Riding). In Scotland the Register of Sasines, held in the Scottish Record Office, performs the same function.

If your ancestors lived or worked on the estate of a local landowner, or on land owned by the Crown, it is always worth checking to see if **Estate Records** survive. These may be found in record offices, solicitors' offices or still in the possession of the landowner's family. **Manorial Records**, where they survive, can also be an extremely valuable source of information, particularly if you find a reference to your ancestor occupying copyhold land.

Details of the whereabouts of surviving collections of Estate and Manorial Records can be ascertained from The Historical Manuscripts Commission, Quality House, Quality Court, Chancery Lane, London WC2A 1HF.

Introduction to Reading Old Title Deeds, 2nd edition, Julian Cornwall. FFHS, 1997.

Using Manorial Records, Mary Ellis. PRO Publications, 1994.

Maps

These can be of immense value in your researches. Some are on a large enough scale to include details of individual buildings and field names. Those you are likely to encounter in your local record office or library include **Enclosure Award** maps (mostly drawn between 1760-1860), **Tithe Maps** (generally between 1836-1854) and **Estate Maps** (see Estate Records above). Also look out for **County Maps, Road Maps and Ordnance Survey Maps** (especially reprints of the New Series dating from the 1840s); remember that those drawn before about 1830 will be of most use to you as they will record the countryside as your ancestors knew it, before railways and motorways destroyed or distorted the communications network which dated from mediaeval times.

Maps for Family History, William Foot. PRO Publications, 1994.

Maps & Plans for the Local Historian & Collector, David Smith. Batsford, 1988.

Local Historian's Encyclopaedia and ***Family Historian's Enquire Within*** (both mentioned previously) include useful sections dealing with maps.

Quarter Sessions

In England and Wales Justices of the Peace were, from the 14th century onwards, required by law to meet four times a year. At these sessions they dealt with most aspects of local life and many of your ancestors may be named in the records whether as criminals, witnesses, taxpayers, debtors or dissenters. Records, which can be voluminous, will be found in CROs (some of the early ones were founded to house these very records). Ask in advance what is available, whether a guide has been published and whether the records are indexed. In Scotland, for similar records, try the local sheriff court or commissary court or, centrally, the Court of Session.

Quarter Sessions Records for Family Historians: A Select List, 4th edition, Jeremy Gibson. FFHS, 1995.

Don't forget other possibilities:

Coroners' Records: see Gibson Guide with same title for details.

East India Company: records held in London in British Library Oriental & India Office Collections.

Electoral Registers and Poll Books: see Gibson Guides for details. Former began in 1832 and list those entitled to vote in parliamentary elections; latter give those who voted in such elections before 1872 (secret ballot introduced).

Emigration and Immigration records: principally in Public Record Office.

Freemen's Records: for many cities lists of these will be found in the local record office or library. Those for London are in the Guildhall Library.

Internet

The Internet has already been mentioned on page 19 but the rapid increase both in the number of people using it and in its coverage of records of assistance to the family historian justifies this further mention.

If you have decided to use a computer and connect to the Internet, it becomes a very good way of publicising your family interests. Some publishers of family history packages provide free storage space on the Internet for information from their users, and automatic ways of preparing information for Internet access once you have keyed it in to the package. This process has become surprisingly easy. Alternatively, when you subscribe to the Internet via a service provider, you usually receive some space on which you can publish information as pages you design yourself. You can then announce it via the Internet, so that anyone making a search for 'genealogy' or 'family history', and any surname included in your pages, will be told your Internet address.

Many of the organisations mentioned in this book – including some family history societies – have their own Web pages; addresses for these can mostly be found in ***The Genealogical Services Directory*** mentioned in the Bibliography to Chapter 5. The sections in that chapter on the Public Record Office and Scotland will also give some idea of the range of information which is rapidly becoming available on the Internet.

CHAPTER FIFTEEN

Presenting Your Researches

It is important to realise that a recital of names, generation by generation, giving dates of birth, marriage and death, although no doubt interesting as a genealogy, is inadequate as a family history. Do not, I urge you, simply become an ancestor collector. Try and build upon the 'skeleton' of the basic information by placing the family events you have discovered into their broader historical context, which will involve investigation of the character and development of the area in which your ancestors lived. The sources suggested in this book will help you to do this.

Eventually you will have accumulated sufficient information to present a coherent account of your findings. Do not keep your discoveries to yourself. Someone, somewhere, may be waiting for a vital piece of evidence, which you have, and someone else may have just the piece of the jigsaw which you need! The easiest way of informing other family historians about your findings is to write an article for the magazine of a Family History Society or for one of the commercial publications. Editors are always looking for suitable material and they will be glad to give advice about presentation. In addition to the results, your methods of research may be of interest to others faced with similar problems.

Family History News & Digest, the half yearly publication of the FFHS, contains a ***Digest*** section summarising most articles which have appeared in the journals of its members. This, coupled with the exchange of journals between Societies, ensures a wide coverage for your article and you could find yourself exchanging information to your mutual benefit with a reader half a world away. In due course the information accumulated may be far more than can be conveniently summarised within the confines of a single article and a larger publication should be considered.

If your forte is the spoken, rather than the written, word you might instead prefer to give a talk to a Society located where your ancestors lived. If you do embark on this, thorough preparation is necessary, particularly with the production of visual material, which is essential for any talk lasting longer than 20 minutes.

Even if you do not feel able to pursue any of the options outlined above, try to share your researches with others by registering the names you are researching with the appropriate Family History Society and by entering them into the various publications mentioned in Chapter 4.

You are warned that this pastime is addictive and may occupy your leisure hours for the rest of your life. May I wish you 'good hunting'.

Bibliography

Writing & Publishing Your Family History, John Titford. FFHS, 1996.

Index

Index